Using a simple yet pow
performance, Karen and ▪ ▪ ▪ ▪ ▪ ▪ ▪
sports to help organisations maintain and increase the performance of their people. The power of recovery has never been more important in today's fast-paced world of work and this book is a must for anyone interested in, or experiencing, burnout or lack of focus. It offers practical solutions for improving efficiency and fast-tracking you to your outcomes.

    – Vicky Smith, researcher, organisational
      psychologist and author of *Brave New Leader*

Rest. Practise. Perform. will be a great tool for organisations to take ideas from to use within their teams. As athletes we are taught very early on about good rest and recovery strategies to enable our bodies to perform at the highest level. It is not sustainable to perform at your peak all year round; recovering is vital both physically and mentally. Sometimes overcomplicating things causes problems within a team environment also. We are taught good routine and back-to-basics that enable our bodies to function at their best: good food, sleep, sunlight and even enjoying hobbies where you can completely switch off. All of these strategies are a great foundation within a team environment and I believe this book with really help organisations see the way sports teams could help them to be even more successful in many areas.

    – Kylie Grimes MBE

As a keen player and spectator of both tennis and football, as well as an organisational leader, this book is a great read but also resonates with my experiences, both at work and in sport. Taking learnings from top sporting performance and applying them to the business world is something I've started to implement now. I'm already seeing results in helping top performers to maintain and reach peak performance at the right times.
   – Simon Bouton, VP global operations and
     experience, Google DeepMind

This book is a game changer... fast-tracking lessons learnt from elite sport and taking them to the world of business. It should be in every business leader's toolbox. As an elite athlete, over the course of my entire career I have learnt the value of rest, high quality practice and performing at the right time. I wish I had read this book sooner!
   – Aaron Phipps MBE, paralympic champion

Rest. Practise. Perform.

What elite sport can teach leaders about sustainable wellbeing and performance.

KAREN MEAGER
AND JOHN MCLACHLAN

Rest. Practise. Perform.
ISBN 978-1-915483-27-0 (paperback)
eISBN 978-1-915483-28-7

Published in 2024 by Right Book Press
Printed in the UK

Contents

Foreword

Karen Meager

In many ways this book is the natural culmination of many years of research and practical experimentation. We didn't plan to write it but increasingly felt that such a book was needed. Our first two books, *Real Leaders* and *Time Mastery*, covered what we considered to be the core challenges that organisations face in the modern world: leadership and time management. The world of work has changed so much in the past few decades. However, despite the best intentions of CEOs, senior leaders and HR professionals, some of the fundamental aspects of running an organisation, leading and organising people, remained a seemingly unsolvable problem.

Our backgrounds are in industry and clinical psychology. I worked my way through various management and leadership roles in retail before landing in the fund management industry. I became fascinated by how people operate, and learned how to support them to do their best work. Then I took my interest in human nature and behavioural change further and trained as a clinical psychotherapist with every intention of pursuing a career in clinical practice. John was a partner in an accountancy firm and a group financial director. He spent his working life trying to bring together people, finances and strategy, which wasn't an easy endeavour!

Even before we met, we had the same ideas and values around learning and growth. We had both separately sought a variety of personal growth experiences through learning about psychology, therapy and hypnotherapy. For a while we pursued independent careers. I worked as a psychotherapist in private practice and gained experience in the NHS, and John combined a role as a business consultant and strategy advisor with a private practice as a hypno-therapist and executive coach. We were both surprised to find that we missed organisational life and started working together to bring our clinical knowledge back into business. We understood that the personal growth field was often too scary, weird and not practical enough for many people, especially those working in organisa-tions 15 years ago. We set about bringing together the latest academic thinking with applied psychology and making it practical and easy to implement. Combining a deep understanding of everyday organisational frus-trations and challenges with our clinical psychology qualifications, we set out to help organisations build and maintain healthy and productive cultures and ways of working. Writing our books was a way of consolidat-ing our ideas, reaching more people and continually improving the quality of our work.

People we spoke to who'd read the first two books gave us consistent feedback, such as 'A life changer for my personal growth and development – but can you help me solve some of my systemic organisational problems?' CEOs wanted solutions they could apply to their whole organisation, leaders and managers wanted something they could trial with their teams, and small business owners wanted a ready-made template they could easily put into place.

We were delighted that employee health and wellbeing were increasing in prominence in the mainstream and industry press, as we'd been advocating for and working in this area for at least 15 years. However, we also heard real concern from leaders about some of the advice that came with this. It seemed that to be a good employer, people needed more flexibility, more time off and more autonomy. Many leaders were concerned about how to balance this and achieve their organisational goals. Could organisations really be both productive and healthy or were they doomed to be high pressure and exhausting environments *and* productive or nice places to work but slow to deliver or ultimately unsuccessful? The message coming from leaders on the ground was 'What about performance?'

Having worked with hundreds of organisations over the years, we knew that it was possible to be both successful and prioritise employee wellbeing. We'd seen it and helped organisations to do it. However, until we started to receive feedback on the previous two books, our work was high touch and bespoke. At the time it was hard to generalise about our work to the point where it could be widely useful. But the call for the third book kept coming, so we went back into academia to see what it could offer us. I continued my research into burnout, particularly burnout prevention and recovery, and John homed in on performance. He found the field of organisational performance dry and limiting, understandably so as even defining performance in organisations was practically impossible. So he looked beyond organisations and landed in the field of elite sports, where there was a lot of excellent research. As his research progressed, he found much that organisations could leverage. In fact, what John learned about sports performance reflected aspects of the bespoke work we were already doing with organisations.

We often joke that John's academic work was a lot sexier than mine. I would mention my burnout research to CEOs and elicit sober, sympathetic nods about how noble and important it was. When I mentioned John was researching performance in elite sports their eyes lit up and suddenly John's diary was full of leaders wanting to discuss his research. Everyone had reflections and suggestions; leaders would come back to work on Monday and discuss what they could learn from the football or tennis they'd watched over the weekend. Our clients started conducting their own experiments based on their favourite sport. Finally, we'd found a foundation that made sense and worked.

Over the past few years, we've tried and tested the 'rest, practise, perform' approach, refining it and making it practically and widely useful. The concept is simple but the application is far from easy. We've touched on our research at the beginning of the book but our focus in writing it has been to make it practical, something you feel you can implement and maintain.

We wanted readers to know how to apply the concepts and overcome some of the most common challenges.

Personally, I've found exploring the world of sport in depth a surprising delight. I used to believe that elite sportspeople were either naturally gifted, lucky or masters of self-torture. I admired them without really understanding them. However, I've come to learn what it takes to perform at an elite level for many years and just how much it's possible for organisations and everyone working in them to apply these principles in their own fields (and even lives) with great results. John and I hope you enjoy the book.

Introduction

Rest, practise, perform: a sustainable rhythm that leads to performance

To be successful, organisations need to perform. The concept of organisational performance has been much discussed and debated but we believe it's generally poorly understood and executed. We find that organisational focus tends to be on 100 per cent performance, where success means everyone must be in maximum performance mode every hour of the working day. This is neither true nor sensible. It is, though, understandable as the need to be productive constantly hangs over leaders. From our vantage point, this mindset results in exhausted teams and often mediocre outcomes. What's more, those outcomes are achieved only through Herculean effort rather than the efficient use of skills, processes and structures that lead to excellence. We think it's time to stop, stand back and look at organisational performance through a new lens.

In elite sports, the goal is to perform at key times. Professional athletes don't expect to perform 24/7. They and their teams design a rhythm to ensure maximum performance in the performance window. Rest and practice are at the heart of this rhythm. In addition to allocating sufficient time for rest and practice, elite sports design these phases to ensure performance is optimal once they're in the performance window. In this book, we'll show you how the rest, practise, perform approach can be applied to your organisation to make it both successful and sustainable.

As a leader, you're likely to have experienced the challenge of trying to consistently deliver at pace. The desire to deliver is nearly always well intended; you probably work in a good organisation that's trying to achieve the right things in the right way. Despite that, your employees may well be exhausted and demotivated, resulting in things moving more slowly than they need to. You may well feel as if you're on a constant hamster wheel. At best, you move forward incrementally each year. However, you may feel that the effort you need to invest to achieve that is dispro-portionate to the result.

If you think about the word 'organisation' for a moment, it means how resources are organised to achieve a certain purpose. In many organisations, people form a large part of those resources. This holds true even though recent innovations have resulted in technology and AI becoming increasingly important for all organisations. People still set the direction, drive the goals and coordinate the essential activities to deliver the strategy. Therefore how you organise your people remains a necessary though complex component of organisational performance. We think it's amazing that many organisations are still relatively successful despite how they organise themselves. But as you've probably seen or experienced, there are many examples of organisations that collapse like a house of cards when the environment in which they operate changes. It's easier for organisations to be successful on a rising tide of a market or innovation. However, when the tide turns, it exposes all the weaknesses and limitations in the system, leaving the organisation vulnerable. We find that companies that can organise themselves well are much more likely to avoid these disastrous consequences.

Employee burnout has become a global issue. Research suggests that systemic limitations and weaknesses in organisations are contributing to this so-called epidemic. Many countries are currently looking at an exhausted, demotivated workforce. Recent research claims that burnout is costing organisations in the UK around £3.7 billion annually in lost working days and decreased productivity (Foy et al 2019). In research conducted before the Covid pandemic, estimates of burnout rates across Europe varied between 10 and 25 per cent in organisations, whereas in caring professions the numbers could be more than 60 per cent (Aronsson et al 2017). Studies conducted since the pandemic indicate that things are only getting worse (Konkel & Heffernan 2022). We speak to leaders who are concerned and want to turn the tide but are struggling to find practical ways to address the problem.

Our research and experience suggest that cultural issues in organisations are exacerbating the problem.

Much of this is unintentional; an organisation's leadership team rarely sets out to exhaust people. However, a combination of factors can quickly lead to a vicious circle of lack of achievement and exhaustion. For example, if people lack clarity, direction and support, there will be a lot of busy but ineffective work going on as people try to prove their worth. To compound the issue, if this work is not valued by the organisation, people become more despondent and demotivated. Tired people think less clearly and make poorer-quality decisions. They struggle to remain emotionally regulated, which is the ability to experience emotions proportionately. This reduced emotional regulation impedes their ability to communicate appropriately, leading to increased confusion and reduced trust. When people aren't clear on what to do to perform well, they often work compulsively, making them even more tired. Consequently, organisations are becoming even less effective. As a result, increasingly gruelling efforts are made by some people to get work over the line, completing the vicious circle. Feeling tired just reading this? We believe there must be a better way.

While there are examples of organisations that buck this trend and are exemplars, they're rare and usually small. It's arguably easier to detect and correct issues in smaller organisations. To find a solution that works better at scale, we suggest looking beyond organisations to a world where wellbeing and performance go hand in hand: the world of sport.

The relevance of sports performance to organisations

Performance is the ultimate outcome in sport. Given that organisations also need to perform, we believe sports provide a worthy and practical comparison. The challenge in making such a comparison, however, is that it can become oversimplified and easy to dismiss as irrelevant. Deeper comparisons require a willingness to study how elite sports work, with an understanding of how organisations themselves work and where they don't. In this book, we'll identify the essential components of performance that elite sports employ and translate them into organisational terms that you can adapt and apply in your work.

In our experience, the core problem for organisations is that it's nearly impossible to define performance in any meaningful way. When we set out to define organisational performance, it seemed a sensible first step to read what academia has to say on the subject. We were left feeling disappointed. This is not to criticise the academic work on organisational performance as a lot of good research has been conducted but it's often focused on a specific, narrow aspect that isn't easily applicable. Additionally, such is the complexity of organisations that there are many alternative factors contributing to performance challenges. After reading hundreds of papers, the summary seems to be that organisational performance is complex and there are many potential dependencies. We found that there's no clear agreed definition of what performance is, even among academics (Sethibe & Steyn 2015; Sfreddo et al 2021). There are also very few studies on the enablers of performance in organisations. Overall we discovered that organisational studies indicate a wide range of potential factors, including good leadership, motivation, employee autonomy and learning mindset (Almatrooshi et al 2016). But if you're looking for useful knowledge that you can apply practically in your organisation to define performance, you'll end up in a dead end.

Without a clear definition of performance, you can't design your activities for success. Sports research clearly defines performance and gravitates around the concept of sustainable performance and the health and fitness of professional sportspeople over time (Supej & Spörri 2021), exploring the complex dynamics between consistent performance and health. It considers concepts that are also relevant to organisations such as leadership, team dynamics and communication. Additionally, sports research is years ahead of organisations in understanding areas such as the impact of physical and mental fitness, nutrition, team cohesion and focused goals on sustainable performance (Fletcher & Arnold 2011; Supej & Spörri 2021). You could argue that the performance element in sport is simple and that makes it easier to focus on – for example, win a league, a match, a race – and you'd be right. However, if organisations spent less time on busy but pointless work and took the time to define what performance means in their business, they could also create an approach that would set them up for success.

The field of sports is regularly quoted as a useful comparison for organisations. Sports professionals are commonly employed as motivational speakers and advisors. However, we've found that organisations can struggle to translate their advice practically and end up with a lot of high-level hints and tips. When advice is too general, it's of limited use to you as a leader in an organisation. Leaders frequently have a good sense of what they need to do but struggle with how to do it. To get a deeper understanding of how elite sports deliver sustainable performance, it's necessary to dig deeper into some tangible examples. Therefore we selected three sports to research in depth.

The three sports we studied were professional tennis, Formula 1 racing (F1) and professional football. These sports are different in many ways but there are also many similarities. Tennis is chiefly about individual performance. F1 is a collective team sport in which there are distinct roles and responsibilities that happen at different times. Football, on the other hand, is a sport that requires the team to work together simultaneously. There are undoubtedly other sporting examples that would provide useful insights and many were considered and discarded for the purpose of researching this book. As authors, we had to consider practical limitations such as access to reasonably detailed (and not overly hyped) first- or second-hand accounts. The chosen sports are well documented and observed, a lot of it first hand by the athletes themselves, but there were also plenty of good quality second-hand accounts written by sports analysts. We also had to consider our own limits of knowledge about other sports. This is why we excluded sports better known to US readers such as baseball and basketball.

The approach for organisational performance

discussed in this book is a result of the study of these sports and the subsequent application of the concepts to organisations. We studied hundreds of hours of documentaries and interviews, read biographies and autobiographies of athletes from the three sports, particularly athletes or teams that had a proven long-term performance record. The relevant themes were lifted for each individual sport, then themes that were consistent across all the sports and could reasonably be considered as contributing factors to performance were grouped together. The themes also needed to be applicable to organisations. Therefore rather than focusing on sport-specific elements such as technique, we focused on the human elements of each sport: teamwork, relational factors, time management and working rhythm, leadership, health, attitude, communication and mindset. We then completed an academic literature review on sports performance and health and cross-checked our results. Finally, we tested our results in real organisations, refining our approach and forming some practical examples and case studies, which we will share with you in this book.

How to use this book

Rest, practise, perform is a rhythm that leads to sustainable performance rather than boom and bust. Each sport we studied uses this rhythm in some form to organise and focus on its people. We found that within these sports, how skilfully teams and individuals are able to follow this rhythm is a significant factor in how well they're able to sustain performance. There's no perfect way to run your team or organisation;

human beings are complex and unpredictable and you won't be able to design your way out of this. However, there are many good ways to run your team or organisation, and this rhythm should be your focus. We believe that small increments in improvement in each of the three areas will positively impact performance. This approach is based on the concept of iteration and development rather than designing something perfect and shooting for it.

The book explores each of these three phases, bringing them to life with sports and organisational examples. We'll suggest ways you can adopt these principles and design them for your team or organisation. If you're not a sports fan, feel free to skip over the sports examples. They're included to illustrate and connect the ideas and concepts and will be insightful and interesting for some, but if even sport isn't your thing, you'll still be able to test and apply the ideas. How you design the rhythm that works for you will be individual to you and your organisation. We'll provide options and perspectives, pros and cons, watch-outs and practical suggestions that you can use as they are, or you can tweak and refine them according to what matters to you. The client and organisational examples are real. They've been used with permission and anonymised to protect confidentiality. For those who want to explore further, there are academic references and links to sources at the end of the book.

We'll now consider the various ways in which the rest, practise, perform rhythm can be applied and some essential questions to think about when applying them to your own organisation. Once you have a high-level shape of what a good rhythm looks like for you, we'll explore the concept of rest, how to avoid burnout, recharge effectively and improve your own resilience as well as your organisation's. Then we'll look at what it means to practise, which is essential but frequently overlooked. Organisations need to do a lot more of this to perform more effectively. Finally, we'll focus on what it means to perform and how to define performance in a tangible way for you and your organisation. The book contains practical suggestions about applying and maintaining performance in your day-to-day work and the importance of celebrating achievements as part of the organisational culture for sustainable performance.

Designing the right rhythm and flow

Before designing the best flow for your team or organisation, start by thinking about what performance means in your organisation. We refer to a 'performance window', which means the specific period that you, your team or your organisation needs to be in full performance mode. To work out what performance means and therefore your performance window, try to think beyond your carefully designed, beautifully worded mission statement. What does your organisation actually do? What is its rhythm? What are the key ebbs and flows of your organisation's year? For example, are you a product company with key launch dates each year or over longer periods, a retail company with important peak sales performance times or a professional services company with a range of clients to support throughout the year? Whatever your organisation does, it will have a natural flow. Building awareness of this will help you design a rhythm of rest, practise and perform that works for you and your organisation.

In doing that, we recommend giving some consideration to what's within your control and what's outside it. This will help you identify the fixed elements that need to be incorporated into the rhythm design. In sport, the rhythm is largely dictated by tournament calendars and there are some elements that the athletes and teams have some control over and others that they don't. This largely depends on the specific sport. Adaptability is required to find the right rhythm and staying within the prescribed boundaries or rules while doing what's necessary to maximise performance. In tennis, players must frequently make a trade-off between attending tournaments that may help them with their ranking positions and getting sufficient physical rest. In Formula 1, the teams can control the process of designing and building their new car each year to improve performance. However, there will also be new technical requirements to meet that are outside their control. In football, clubs have little control over their match timetable.

When considering your own external factors, it's important to ask yourself whether these are real or whether you're making some unhelpful assumptions. You may be assuming limits that you believe to be immovable but can influence. For example, your organisation may have a parent company with general ways of working, particular types of clients with historic wishes and needs or a certain board meeting cadence and feel that these are fixed and outside your control. This assumption may be worth challenging. We often find that, when explored, leaders have more flexibility and influence over these and many other areas than they originally thought. The more flexibility you can identify and utilise, the better. It will allow you to have more day-to-day control over what happens to you, your team and organisation and enable you to identify what you need to do to optimise for performance.

The first step is to take the time to fully understand your external factors. Speak to key people to understand the dependencies. Map out your assumptions about these external factors and actively challenge them. We find it's common to discover that seemingly fixed meetings were originally scheduled for a reason that's no longer relevant. You may also find that your belief that certain people are wedded to certain ways of working is untrue or that client deadlines are just old habits. There will be events and deadlines that are planned with good reason or are genuinely out of your control; the key is to know the difference between the real reasons and the assumptions you're making. Once you're clear on the factors outside your control, you can begin to map out your optimal rest, practise, perform rhythm. The three elements are introduced briefly below and each will be explored in detail throughout the book.

Rest

Relax – this doesn't mean putting your feet up all the time, providing sleep pods for your employees or granting extended holidays to everyone! But you can, of course, do these things if you wish, providing they support performance and provide the right kind of respite from whatever energy has been expended through performing.

The purpose of the rest phase is to recharge and regain any resources lost through the performance window. This can take several forms and needs careful design and communication, otherwise people won't know what to do with this time. Humans are so addicted to activity nowadays that it's hard to get them to stop. Or, dare we say it, even get yourself to stop? Everyone rests in different ways and there are even types of rest that can be counterproductive. We'll share specific suggestions for ways in which you as a leader and your organisation can help people rest appropriately to support overall performance. For the moment, though, think about when the rest phase begins for your team or organisation. This is usually immediately after they have performed. For some that will mean the end of the delivery of a project or peak season of activity. For some it will be built into their day or week, which is common for professions where you need to perform every day. This could mean a day free from client meetings each week for client-facing individuals or teams, or sections of the day away from intense work – whatever it takes to help people to recharge and get ready to practise. You and your teams don't need to be 'always on' – honestly, you don't.

Practise

The purpose of the practise phase is to train, learn and get ready to perform. In sport this phase is arguably the most straightforward to design, given the skills and techniques required for elite sports performance. However, it's not always so clear cut. Sports such as F1 and tennis have only recently included strength training and general conditioning as part of the practise phase. The importance of overall fitness for sustaining performance in any sport has become more obvious, enabling athletes to perform later in life to high standards and avoid injury. Furthermore, the explosion of sports psychology, mindset coaches and the increasing number of elite sportspeople talking about their mental health challenges shows the importance of focusing on mental as much as physical wellbeing in the practise phase.

In our view, organisations traditionally struggle with this phase, often expecting people to perform immediately with a few short pieces of training and some cursory onboarding when people join. Additionally, there appears to be a notion in organisations that they need to perform all the time, which is both unrealistic and unhelpful. When designing this phase, consider what technical skills and non-technical skills and abilities are needed. Non-technical abilities require special consideration because we believe they're a critical lever when it comes to performance. These abilities and skills are less obvious but make the world of difference to an organisation's performance. Without them, much unnecessary time and effort is wasted in putting right things that didn't need to go wrong in the first place. Leadership development is one practice that organisations often discard as unnecessary or needing too much time investment, which then becomes a huge cost in difficult times or when up against a well-developed competitor.

Perform

In the performance window, you're doing all you can to achieve your goal. This requires focus and intensity, so it's essential that you know what you're aiming for. In sport, this is where matches, medals and tournaments are won and lost. The competition is also clear, as they're literally next to you on the grid or standing on the other side of the net. We appreciate that this can be less clear in business; you may have a direct competitor but you may also be competing in a specific market context or economy or even against your own previous year's performance. Therefore it's even more important to clearly define your benchmark of success. In sport this phase is short relative to the practise phase. In F1, cars spend six hours in total on the track over a race weekend; tennis matches last no more than a few hours at most; and football games are timed at 90 minutes. Consider the time your organisation is spending in the practise phase relative to your performance window.

Organisations can be quite adept, dare we say practised, at explaining that they need performance 24 hours a day, usually with a long list of reasons, justifications and excuses. We suggest that a lot of this work is not performance. People often feel they need to articulate it this way for fear that it won't otherwise be valued and that's understandable. This is where organisations need to have the courage to change their collective mindset or they'll end up with a workforce working flat out on things that don't really matter. Sadly, that's the reality in a lot of organisations today.

The sports perspective

Let's look at how the three sports use the rest and practise phases as essential elements of their performance.

Formula 1

In F1 there's a 14-day break over the summer, which is enforced in the regulations. No technical development work on the cars is allowed during this period and only a few clearly defined operations remain open. This is partly an attempt to preserve a level playing field across teams but also to give teams much-needed time to rest and recuperate from the punishing racing schedule. It's not just a nice thing to do. The impact of run-down and exhausted strategists, technicians and drivers with an F1 car in their hands could literally be fatal and not just for their own team. This is why it's imposed industry wide.

In F1, the practise phase is a whole team effort, with drivers involved at every stage. While everyone has their clear areas of expertise, this phase involves many mini cycles of testing and iterating to try to isolate the optimal state for the race weekend. F1 tends to operate in a similar cadence across all teams, with certain days and times for media and on-track practice sessions, for example. In such an intense team environment, this level of top-down planning and attention to practice sessions enables maximum focus on what will help the team to perform.

Football

In football, professional games are organised into three key phases: pre-season, when friendly games are played for training and practice purposes; in season, when the main competition is played; and off season, when there are no official matches. This schedule is primarily designed to work around the weather and international tournaments. This kind of rhythm is clearly a rest (off season), practise (pre-season), perform (season) cycle but many teams run this model in micro cycles throughout the season, with designated rest days and training days, all leading up to the next big competitive match.

Tennis

In professional tennis, the rhythm is centred around the four grand slam tournaments – the Australian Open, US Open, Wimbledon (UK) and French Open, which are spread throughout the year. However, there are many other tournaments and if players were to play them all, they would only get four weeks off a year. Therefore tournaments are ranked in terms of prize money and ranking points so that players can design a rhythm that works for their ambitions, experience and career stage, while maximising attendance. Some are mandatory for top players and some are optional. It's a logistical headache but tour organisers construct the calendar intentionally to make it a bit easier for the players and their teams, for example holding smaller tournaments in a particular part of the world, leading to the major open tournament in one cycle, called a 'swing'. This enables players to stay in that region, minimise travel, acclimatise to the weather and focus.

Applying the rest, practise, perform approach to organisations

Organisations differ from each other in many ways but they usually have one thing in common. A critical factor to the success and profitability of most organisations is how they organise and coordinate their people. As you consider what rhythm would work best for your organisation, reflect on the following questions.

Who are the 'performers' in your organisation?
We don't mean who's performing well, as that can be in any role. Which role or roles are the ones that determine the success of your organisation? In a service organisation, it could be the people who provide the service to the client. Examples include the architect in an architectural practice, front-line carers in a healthcare organisation or technical engineers in an innovative technology company. In these situations, it's a straightforward question to answer but there are organisations where identifying the performer roles is less obvious.

Take a retailer, for example. You could argue that your performer roles are the shop staff or online service representatives (or the quality of your online bot) but the answer really lies in your value proposition. If your differ-entiating factor is your product, then your designers could be your key performers. If your differentiating factor is range, then your buying team could be your key performers. If your differentiating factor is your price, then your negotiating team could be your key performers.

In an innovative technical organisation, the key performers in the organisation could shift over time. At the early stages researchers could be key performers but at a later stage the key performer status could shift to your technical engineers, who need to build the thing your researchers have designed. Later it may move to the team whose responsibility it is to sell it and make sure it enters the world problem free. For some organisations the key performer roles will be static but in some they will shift and it's important to consider that when designing your rhythm. If you're designing for a division or team rather than a whole organisation, we suggest the same principle applies. The rhythm you create should enable the key performer roles to be at their peak when you need them to be. That's not to say that other roles are less important. They're critical to the performance of this key role because everything is connected; there's no point in having the best striker in the world if they can't get the ball.

Are there any external factors outside your sphere of control that you need to consider?
Examples include regulatory deadlines, customer cycles or seasonal periods. These are the times when you may need to focus on performing and they can support you in designing your organisational rhythm, allowing you to plan in your rest and practise periods. Retailers have obvious seasonal cycles to plan. Therefore if you provide customer service training for retailers, those cycles may be good rest and practise periods for your organisation while your customers are busy performing. Accountants and investment professionals have externally driven regulatory deadlines. Product organisations work in project-based cycles. If these organisations are your customers, where do you

fit into this? There's no point in being available when you're not needed.

Where would more practice improve your performance?
Identify the skills and capabilities you need to ensure your key performer roles are performing to their best. This includes training in role-specific technical skills and personal development skills around mindset, attitudes, communication and leadership. The practise phase is also crucial to resolving recurring issues or problems that impact performance in your team or organisation. Organisations have retrospectives and post-mortems to help improve performance and while these can be useful, they can miss the key elements that created the issue. There's a focus on what went wrong or didn't happen and then processes are put in place to minimise the likelihood of it recurring. This can result in more time-consuming processes. Asking why something went wrong is likely to be more effective as it will help you identify a root cause. You can then identify what you need to practise to avoid this happening in the future.

The practise phase can include testing ideas and piloting new initiatives and is a valuable exercise for many organisations. However, in the desire to launch new ideas, processes or services quickly, all too often this step is skipped for fear that it's a waste of time or money. If you're an organisation that starts a lot of shiny things that don't last, then you probably need to do more testing or piloting.

Design your rhythm

Once you've identified the key building blocks of your organisational needs and challenges using the questions above, you can begin to design a rhythm that works for you and your team or organisation. Here are a few organisational examples to get you thinking.

Design to a client rhythm

A service company has a completely remote workforce and has invested time in creating a rhythm that works for them and their business. In their rest phases, when client demand is low, they organise twice yearly retreats for the team to bond and regroup. The retreats are held in hotels in beautiful locations around the world to maximise the ability of the team to rest and are seen as a good return on investment for this relatively small business. The retreats are deliberately loose in structure, with only a small amount of organised group work. The CEO is careful to avoid the temptation to pack in too much for these occasions as this would limit or negate the purpose. In the practise phase, which is roughly a month after each retreat, the team experiments with and refines new ideas based on customer feedback collated in the previous six months as well as their own ideas.

They experiment with ways to improve delivery of the service, trial new service suggestions, get client feedback and iterate. This is also a time for the team to undertake professional development. Their performance window is based on client demand and their main clients are professional service organisations. For around nine months of the year, they're primarily in perform mode, focusing on delivering consistent quality of service during periods of high demand. During the performance window, the team implement small cycles of rest and practice throughout the week by having a day each week to read, reflect, recuperate, meet each other for coffee or prepare.

Design to project cycles

In an architectural practice, the key performers (the architects) are all working on different projects with varying project cycles. Client demands create significant pressure to respond quickly to time-sensitive priorities at key stages of the projects. They were concerned about the stress this was putting on the team and sought to create a rhythm that could more sustainably manage these demands. Therefore the rhythm is run in project groups where the lead project manager designs a workflow that matches the client's needs and reduces the stress on the team.

As project teams aren't static and are only pulled together for the purpose of one project (which can last years, depending on size and complexity), the team bond forms part of the practise phase and projects start in this part of the cycle. Time is spent upfront bonding as a team and learning about each other's ways of working. This usually happens immediately after a contract is agreed. Some of the team members are in the scoping phase of the project and it's a good time to work together to trial different options and alternatives as a group. Notice that the team bonding is more active than when in the rest phase (as in the service company); the work is more geared towards the capabilities that will be necessary to deliver the project. The performance window happens in two stages, one where the final plans are presented to the client and the second being the delivery of the building. There's usually a short rest and practise phase between the two. Once the project is finished there's an extended rest phase where people take proper holidays and work on their own general professional development, complete project reviews and celebrate.

Test your design

Once you have a high-level rhythm in mind, you'll want to test it. There are always nuances and things that need tweaking or flexing. Having a rhythm doesn't mean it's rigid but you can and should always return to your rhythm when you're able to. While the ideal would always be to maintain your rhythm, this isn't a reality for most people working in organisations. It's all too easy and understandable for an individual, team or organisation to lose their rhythm because of work pressures, challenging trading issues or other environmental factors. A tennis player with an injury or a young family may do as few non-mandatory tournaments as possible for a few seasons and then get back on track. A new football manager may need to spend more time in the practise phase with their team at the beginning, knowing it will pay off later. Once you've established a rhythm that works most of the time for your team or organisation, you can flex when needed. However, if you're flexing too often or by too much, it's probably your rhythm that needs adjustment.

As a rule, the performance window should be shorter compared to the rest and practise phases. This is especially true if performing itself is intense. Try to be careful in equating performance with work. People are still working when they're resting and practising. Professionals frequently train for many years to obtain qualifications and this fits in with the practise phase, except maybe the performance required for those all-important exams.

We'll now move on to explore each of the phases in more depth. For each phase, we'll encourage you to consider what you can do for yourself, your team or your organisation in each of the three phases. First, pull up your favourite duvet because it's time to talk about rest.

Chapter 1
The rest phase

Rest is a conscious activity. Stress and tension build up in your body unconsciously. None of us decide to be stressed or overwhelmed; it often happens outside our awareness. Therefore we all need to be aware of how and when we rest. The rest phase isn't necessarily about putting your feet up, binge-watching Netflix or going on holiday, although all of these and more may help. To make the most of it, we believe rest needs to be deliberate, planned and thought through, as many people don't fully appreciate the purpose of the rest phase and why it can help them perform better. Therefore it's about doing something different, changing the activity you or your team are engaged in and recharging so that in future you can perform in a sustainable way.

The impact of stress and therefore the need for rest is much talked about, particularly as burnout rates rise across the world. Burnout is the most prominent and most frequently identified consequence of a lack of conscious rest in the world of work. We've noticed that the impact on individuals, organisations and performance remains grossly underestimated in most organisations. Building rest phases into the organisation goes beyond being kind to your employees; it's a key component of business success and has a significant impact on business profitability. To understand why integrating rest is essential to performance and to help you plan the most effective types of rest for you and your team, let's look at the most critical components of burnout and its impact on individuals and organisations.

Burnout

The concept of burnout first emerged in the 1970s and yet it was only in 2019 that the World Health Organization included a detailed classification of burnout in the 11th revision of the International Classification of Diseases (ICD-11). Burnout is generally defined as a stress-induced syndrome explained by three key dimensions: emotional exhaustion, depersonalisation and reduced personal efficacy (Maslach et al 2001).

In the emotional exhaustion dimension of burnout, people will have symptoms such as fatigue, extreme overwhelm and feeling unable to cope with a job they would normally be able to function well in. When experiencing depersonalisation, it's common for people to distance themselves from work and colleagues. There's an increasing cynicism towards work or an impatience or resentment towards the human aspects of work such as collaboration or management. People also report lacking a feeling of achievement, which might be real or imagined. When experiencing burnout people may develop a compulsive attitude to work, working long hours to overcome a perceived lack of achievement. The condition tends to have a gradual onset, resulting in adrenal burnout, which is defined as an almost complete loss of energy and a major psychophysical breakdown. While the peak of this condition can pass quite rapidly, people can experience the physical and psychological repercussions for an average of two to four years.

While burnout has some symptoms in common with conditions such as depression or anxiety, which impact all areas of a person's life, burnout is seen as a relationship primarily with work. The build-up of burnout can take place over months or even years and the well-documented 'denial phase' of burnout means that it's often a challenge for people to acknowledge what's happening to them (Finan et al 2022). To add to this, most academic research in the field is predominantly focused on the causes and impact of burnout rather than recovery (Ahola et al 2017). Recovery times are generally underreported but are estimated to be between three and 18 months (Ahola et al 2017; Pijpker et al 2021). Anyone who has experienced burnout knows how dreadful it is. Anyone in a leadership position who sees the knock-on impact not only on the individual but the whole team would agree that avoiding instances of burnout where possible and helping people to recover well from intense periods of work is worth the time and effort.

Yet in the everyday busyness of business and with endless deadlines, it can be hard to prioritise the things that we all know we need to do to stay well and resilient.

That's partly why building rest into your team or organisational rhythm is so important. By building it in, you don't have to hope and pray that people are taking care of themselves, because some respite is integrated into the system and ways of working. The limited research focused on burnout recovery indicates that a combination of individual and contextual factors is the most effective (Salminen et al 2017). As a leader or manager, you can help address some of the contextual factors. All good employee wellbeing reasons aside, though, there's also a simple but powerful reason to include a rest phase into your cycle: well-rested people perform better.

The right type of rest

Over the years, elite sporting bodies have focused more on rest periods as part of their sporting calendars. Tournaments are carefully planned and consideration is given to the amount of travel athletes are required to make. Even ten years ago, sports professionals had a relatively short period at the top of their chosen sport. Now, more people are playing and competing at the top level for longer. This isn't solely down to rest but it's a significant factor. It's not simply that they rest but that they engage in particular types of rest. We believe this is something organisations can learn a lot from.

Effective rest is to do with resting the thing you're currently using to perform. In sports, this may be your body. If you work in a service or caring industry, you may need emotional rest from people or intense situations. If your day-to-day work involves solving complex technical problems, you may need to rest your brain for a while. We appreciate that this can feel counterintuitive as the part of yourself that's used to perform is usually the part you know best how to use. You'll have created a habit of using your mind or people skills, therefore it's your default mode of operation. However, using a different mode for a period has some powerful benefits.

Our own research into burnout recovery indicated that there were three critical factors for long-term successful recovery from burnout. These factors can also prevent problems arising if they're built into the rest phase.

First, people who broadened their horizons and didn't obsess or focus only on work recovered quickly from burnout. This broadening of horizons can be different for different people. Contrary to what you may expect and the advice that's often given to people with burnout, successful recovery doesn't necessarily mean being idle. Instead, use your rest and recovery time to do something that engages a different part of yourself. For example, you could broaden your horizons by taking up exercise, spending more time outdoors in nature, developing an interest or hobby, spending more (or less) time with other people, or even volunteering. It's not necessarily about working less, just differently.

All too often people create more stress and issues by reducing or simply stopping doing what they know is good for them. This is equally true for organisations. If you're a leader, what have you stopped doing or encouraging that helped your team or organisation to rest and take time out from the need to constantly perform? Keeping simple time boundaries is one thing that slips easily during pressured periods or environments. Everyone knows that working late all the time isn't good for you but the odd late night can lead to another and before you know it, you're working a 50-hour week. Sadly, a lot of those 50 hours will be a waste of time if you're not properly rested. As a leader, you have some responsibility to manage the time boundaries in your team. While people should take responsibility for their own time management, many aren't good at it because of the competitive nature of organisations and the pressure (real or perceived) to deliver.

Building social support both in and out of work is the second factor that accelerates recovery from burnout and is equally important in the rest phase. People who have colleagues they can depend on and trust are less prone to burning out. In healthy teams where trust is high, people are more likely to discuss their issues early and openly, which results in more group problem solving. Making sure that your team communicates positively and gets along well is critical. In addition, addressing people's issues promptly and effectively is probably your biggest mitigator of burnout. If people feel threatened or unsafe at work or feel unable to speak up if they have a problem, they won't perform well. Aside from building social support into ways of working, some organisations have friends and family events that bring people together, creating a sense of community and building social support. These events can be hugely beneficial for some but shouldn't be seen as compulsory. Some people prefer to keep a boundary between work and home, and we believe this should be respected. Compulsory fun, however well intended, won't build social support.

The final factor in successful burnout recovery is helping people to get back in touch with the signals they receive from their body. The research found this to be particularly important where the cause of burnout was mental or emotional exhaustion, as people often deny their own feelings and shut themselves off to keep going. People need to be able to rely on the emotional and physical signals they're getting from their body and when work is generally considered to be a place where emotions aren't welcome, people often repress them, which will likely lead to bigger issues over time. As a leader, you don't need to become the team counsellor. Simply avoiding negative behaviours such as belittling, undermining and teasing and encouraging others to do the same can make a huge difference.

While as an organisation or leader you can't force people to undertake certain activities in their free time, during rest phases you can do things within the organisation that encourage them to rest the part of them that they use to perform. If your team spends their performance window talking to customers, they probably need more reflective activities in their rest phase. These don't need to be frivolous activities: they can be directly beneficial to work while still providing much-needed rest. Here are some examples.

Switching to a different mode

Julie is a call centre leader in an investment company. She used the rest phase for the team to have technical training on investing and stock allocation. It was useful and relevant knowledge but also more reflective training, with some expert speakers and online work. It got them out of their usual performance mode, which was talking. This may seem coun- terintuitive as most trainers would want to encourage engagement and discussion during training. However, if part of the purpose is rest, a different mode is effective. Julie found it provided them with respite, as well as a learning opportunity.

Dileep runs a highly academic team focused on technical problems. They often worked alone in their field of expertise, enjoying the solitary thinking time but also needing to collaborate cross functionally to succeed. They didn't like 'forced fun' so Dileep knew this wouldn't work to encourage rest but he wanted to get them to talk and get to know each other. He arranged for them to go to a series of talks not directly applicable to their work but relevant to the industry. The talks were to do with how their expertise fitted into the wider world. Afterwards, they went for dinner to discuss the talks.

This was beneficial on several fronts. It got them out of their habitual thinking without stressing them out or causing anxiety but still engaged their thinking in a way they appreciated. The discussions helped them to understand each other better and connect more as a working group.

Research suggests that time spent building relationships across levels of the organisation, rebuilding bonds, understanding and even just hanging out together, is essential for the health of the organisation, not just the individuals involved (Jo & Ellingson 2019). Therefore spending time in the rest phase as a team can be highly effective. This can be from simple, short get-togethers at work and speaking events on topics not necessarily connected to the day job, all the way up to having awaydays or longer retreats.

Another potential rest activity that you, as a leader, can consider for you and your team is to invest in personal development. For many people, self-improvement isn't something they think about every day. Research generally supports our belief that organisations that use a rest period to invest in the development of their leaders and managers are likely to become more resilient. They'll experience fewer problems with burnout and organisational health as well as setting the foundation for a healthy culture, which are all essential for high performance. The rest phase isn't a uniform, one-size-fits-all activity. Different organisations will have different cultures and you need to consider and design your rest activities based on what will work for your culture.

That said, there's one universal issue to consider in designing the rest phase. You'll probably have read a lot of articles about the importance of switching off from technology and we'll cover this more in Chapter 3. The reason that habitually using technology is so exhausting is twofold. First, as most people use technology for work, it puts them in a work mindset. Second, socialising via technology disconnects you from people or at best creates superficial connections. Given the importance of building relationships and social connection for organisational health and its relevance in mitigating burnout, the more time people spend in a disconnected state, the worse their social skills and the more disconnected they become. Almost everyone these days relies on technology in some form but we should control it, not the other way around.

Now that the concept and complexities of rest are a little clearer, the next step is to take a deeper look at three specific types of rest in more detail – physical, mental and emotional rest. The following three chapters will take each in turn, considering the different challenges people face if they need rest in these areas and what can be done to support them.

Key takeaways

- ¤ The rest phase is about taking your health and your team's health seriously. When you get older and less mobile, you'll understand just how valuable your health is. Unfortunately, we're all at risk of taking it for granted.
- ¤ While the human body has the capacity for healing and recuperation, you need to be careful not to push it too far.
- ¤ In addition to being bad for individual human beings, lack of physical rest isn't good for performance in organisations. If they're unhealthy, people can become unproductive, develop poor decision-making skills and become unable to think creatively.
- ¤ In organisations, facilitating physical self-care for employees isn't just a nice thing to do – it also makes good business sense.

Chapter 2
Physical rest

Fewer jobs are physically demanding these days but many people are more tired than ever. Human beings used to toil in the fields and do practical tasks all day long, whereas now the most physically demanding thing many professionals do is take themselves off mute or carry their laptop to the next meeting. Given that, for many, the world of work is less physically demanding, why are people so exhausted?

The answer is complex and multifaceted. Perhaps surprisingly, the fact that the benefits of physical activity are no longer present in most people's working lives is an issue. Physical roles enable you to work out your stress through activity. Exercise helps to control your cortisol levels, which can build up in the body, particularly under prolonged periods of stress. If the most physical activity you do is to walk from meeting to meeting, you're unable to provide your body with the opportunities to naturally process the daily stresses of life. Therefore, for some people, more physical activity will provide them with the right type of rest. The answer, of course, is to do your physical activity outside work. However, due to the mental and emotional strains present in today's world of work, people frequently find that they don't have much left in the tank for physical exercise at the end of the working day.

The lack of energy people report at the end of the working day is mostly down to mental and emotional strains, which arise in several ways. One strain is that fewer people feel on top of their workload, having the constant sense that there's always more to do. This is coupled with a personal feeling, if not an organisational expectation, that you will do it. This feeling is heightened further by the 24/7 access via today's technology to your work files and colleagues at home, on the train, on holiday – you get the picture and probably feel the pain. If you have a role where you can stand back at the end of each day and easily see and appreciate what you've achieved, it provides gratification and reduces personal strain. Having to wait longer for projects or pieces of work to come to fruition keeps our bodies in a state of alert for longer, providing little gratification in the here and now.

Another organisational trend impacting the feeling of gratification and adding to the feelings of stress is the apparent requirement to live in a state of constant or regular change. People feel that goals and objectives keep being altered to meet some perceived new need or challenge. Furthermore, the constantly refilling email inbox, messaging services and endless meetings rarely provide a feeling of achievement and gratification. All of this contributes to the overall feeling of not being on top of things. Additionally, burnout rates suggest people are more emotionally invested in their work than they used to be a few decades ago when work was thought of more as a means to an end. This increased emotional investment adds to the emotional strain that people feel. For many people we work with, their role is a vocation that forms a valuable part of their self-worth and identity.

The lack of physical activity in most people's day-to-day work and the modern work environment build up the emotional and mental strain in the body. However, it's worth noting that this isn't the case for everyone. Where people have well-developed boundaries between their work and non-work lives or don't see their work as a significant factor in their identity and self-worth, they don't allow this strain to build. Others view their work as merely a way of earning money and there's nothing wrong with that. They may be less happy when they're doing the work but they leave their work at the door and, as a result, are less emotionally connected to it and therefore less exhausted. These people are at a lower risk of physical exhaustion caused by mental and emotional strain. Arguably this may come at the cost of work fulfilment but that type of fulfilment isn't sought by everyone.

The lack of general physicality in a lot of industries coupled with more complex, longer-term work and regularly changing priorities means that it's harder to know if you're making progress or to see genuine achievements on a regular basis. When it comes to the need for physical rest, this is a toxic combination. People know exercise is good for them but are often too mentally and emotionally exhausted to do it – and so the vicious cycle continues. There are some physical activities in today's world of work but they often don't help with processing stress; in fact, they can add to it.

Examples of this include people standing as they work, which won't process the stress because they're not moving around, and running around the building from meeting to meeting. Again, rather than relieving it, this adds to stress. Additionally, a lot of people endure considerable commutes as well as balancing family logistics, all of which are physically taxing but don't provide stress relief.

As a leader, it would help to build physical rest into the rhythm if the role is physically demanding and build in physical movement if it isn't. This will make it easier for people to integrate healthy practices into their work. In addition, for people in less physically demanding roles, basic physical care should become a priority. Here are some suggestions for ways in which you, as a leader, can build physical rest into your organisational rhythm.

Be mindful of rest and recuperation in periods of travel

If your team needs to travel for work, building in time for rest and recuperation will pay dividends. It may appear unproductive to arrive somewhere the night before or uneconomical to travel business class instead of economy but a tired or unrested employee will not perform at their best. Remember, though, what people find restful is often an individual preference. Some people feel better rested after sleeping at home and getting up early and for some a night in a hotel is the best solution. So it's important to consider that what might work for you won't work for everyone else. When weighing up the benefits versus the costs, consider the performance value of what someone must do at the end of their travels. If this takes place in their performance window, then you'll likely diminish performance by optimising for cost.

Provide opportunities for people to move about during the working day

Some organisations provide excellent facilities for physical exercise but are they well utilised? Can people attend a class without feeling guilty? If you're a leader and fortunate enough to have access to such amenities, plan time for the team to take advantage of it during a rest phase. It might not always be practical to do yoga three times a week during a performance window but during a rest phase this can rise to the top of the priority list. Even if you don't have state of the art facilities, simply encouraging people to move about more can help with physical rest. Avoiding long periods of sitting during meetings and going for short walks while having one-to-one catch-ups can all help if people are used to sitting at desks. It's all about mixing up physical movement so that you're not static for long periods of time. More people than ever work from home now or in a hybrid format but this doesn't necessarily solve the issue. Do you have breaks planned in the day so that people can move about, or do you diarise meetings back to back? Having the opportunity to move is part of physical rest. We suggest considering short breaks between meetings to enable people to move around, visit the toilet or get a drink. Some organisations have 45-minute meetings on work from home days or start all meetings at five past the hour. This all helps people to get away from their screen and move around without worrying about being late or unable to prepare for the next meeting. You might also find your meetings run on time and more effectively as a positive side effect.

Building opportunities for stress release into the team rhythm

Finding ways for the team to process their build-up of stress was a constant challenge for Di. Her team were mainly sitting at desks or in meetings and spent much of their time having intense conversations, especially during the performance window. There was no doubt they cared about their work and were good colleagues but Di found that the atmosphere became like a pressure cooker at times and wasn't sustainable. She put it down to the combination of a stressful job and a lack of movement. Di decided to reorganise the workflow structure so that people had the choice to move more during the rest phase. She shortened the working day (when they were in the office) so that no one was expected to be in the office before 11 am or after 3 pm. This gave people permission to exercise or travel out of peak times. As this wasn't practical during the performance window, she forced more movement by holding the daily stand-ups outside or in a different building. It became a bit of a competition in the team to come up with interesting new places to have the daily stand-up. While this didn't completely resolve the team's build-up of stress, she noticed a significant shift in energy levels; in particular, people seemed to go home with some energy left in the tank.

Coach people to integrate physical movement and rest into their working routines

When people believe you expect them to be constantly available or they're working compulsively, they may need some help to build physical rest into their schedules. As a leader, setting a good example is essential. People will do what you do. They won't do as you say if you're not doing it as well. On top of setting a good example, you can coach people and encourage them to build good physical rest practices into their day. Remember that everyone's different and what works for you might not work for them. That said, simply by sharing, suggesting and encouraging on a consistent basis, you can help people to make small changes that will make a big difference.

Sleep is a fundamental rest that everyone needs. A lot of people understand the need for good quality sleep but still find it difficult to achieve. The distractions and strains of life as well as physical issues and caring responsibilities can get in the way of a good sleeping pattern. If it isn't practically possible to get eight hours a night (although this figure is in dispute by some experts in the field), then encourage people to do what they can to prioritise restorative forms of rest.

Physical rest can also include exercise, as long as this is different from the physical activities you need to do to perform. For someone who rushes about all day, slower, more sedative forms of exercise such as yoga or Pilates are good. For it to qualify as rest, it should be restorative and match what you need. Hot, sweaty exercise with loud music pumping out may not necessarily be what's needed. If someone is quite sedentary during the day, a brisk walk or gentle jog could do them a world of good.

Scaling back the power workout

Matt is the founder of a technology consultancy. The business was growing and he was in constant demand from clients and members of his team. He loved exercise but found that he'd come out of his usual gym workout feeling irritated and unsettled. He was finding it harder to sleep and becoming increasingly tired. When he reflected, he found that this was because pumping iron at the gym left him even more pumped up about his responsibilities and the things he had to do so the adrenaline was flowing. Then he went home and couldn't sleep, which was hardly surprising. For practical reasons he couldn't exercise in the mornings so instead saved his power workouts for the weekends and experimented with different types of exercise such as walking or yoga in the evenings that slowed him down, ready for rest. Once the business stabilised, he went back to his former routine; he just needed to scale it back for a while.

Varying the types of exercise you take will also provide physical rest. If you enjoy exercise, get out of your routine every now and then. If you usually pound the streets, try lifting some weights. If you normally do circuits, try swimming for a period of time. The change of physicality not only engages new muscles you might not have used for a while but it also helps to shift your energy and mindset.

Key takeaways

⌗ While many roles are now not physically demanding, people may still need physical rest in their work.

⌗ In roles where people are physically sedentary, movement will help them to process their stress.

⌗ As a leader you can plan physical rest into your organisation's working rhythm, coach your team to think about physical rest as part of their own working routines and set a good example.

Chapter 3
Mental rest

The overstimulation that many people experience these days is limiting their mental capacity. Your mind processes a huge amount of data every day. What your senses take in through your eyes in terms of social media, instant messages, emails, documents, video calls and through your ears in terms of conversations, meetings and presentations – all this data is being processed through your mind and body. As if that wasn't overwhelming enough, many people's thinking habits don't serve them well. If you're someone prone to overthinking, you'll know it's a problem but can't help yourself. It becomes a habit many people feel controlled by rather than in control of. All these factors contribute to the case for more mental rest.

All the demands on your attention don't help, either. There are a lot of complex problems to solve in the world of work and the ability to think clearly and be able to use your full mental capacity for critical tasks is good for you and good for your organisation. Without mental rest, people become less effective, take longer to achieve things and make poor decisions. We find that, at times, people can become completely overwhelmed and unable to perform at all. This is a terrible situation for the individual and the organisation and we believe it's totally unnecessary.

If you're a leader of a team whose jobs involve intense periods of thinking-based work, you might have a potential performance problem on your hands. You need these people to think at their best. However, some of them are likely to be prone to overthinking habits that can mentally exhaust them, negatively affecting their ability to think and consequently their performance. Even in roles where creative or technical thought isn't the main purpose of the job, anyone using technology in their role still has all the noise of it coming their way, contributing to mental overload. It seems impossible to shut it all off. What's more, human minds can become addicted to it, craving more stimulation. This can result in a vicious cycle of overstimulation and exhaustion, which is why we end up staring at our phones with no idea what we're looking for or at!

Without adequate mental rest, people are also at increased risk of developing mental health problems. According to the mental health charity Mind (2022), one in four people will experience some kind of mental health problem each year. One in six people report experiencing the most common forms of mental health problems, anxiety and depression, each year in England alone. While the reasons behind the development of mental health problems are complex and multilayered, building mental rest into your personal rhythm or, if you're a leader, into your team's rhythm, will help build resilience as well as keep your and your team's thinking abilities at an optimum level to maintain high levels of performance.

Mental rest involves resting your usual mental processes so that they aren't overworked. To do this, it helps to focus on something different to what normally exercises your mental muscles. You'll probably have seen a lot of advice given about what kinds of mental breaks to take; these are all useful but also general-isations. They're unlikely to work for everyone; it all depends on what mental activity you normally engage in. The standard advice is to take deliberate breaks from technology, which works well for people who are surgically attached to their phones or laptops. If, however, you're a personal trainer, reading the news feed on your phone could be the mental rest you need after watching people exercise all day. Think about what kind of mental work you normally do and plan to build different activities into your rhythm to give yourself a mental rest. As a leader, what can you do for your team or organisation to help people take mental rest?

Engage your thinking elsewhere

Mental rest has a lot to do with what people think about when they're mentally resting. If you're not looking at your device but still thinking about that email you need to write, it's not mental rest. On the other hand, it's equally common for people to get caught in the trap of thinking that resting is about 'doing nothing'. Rest is as much about doing something different; it's not about having to sit still or meditate for hours. If you're someone who finds it hard to switch off, try turning your attention to something that engages your brain but isn't related to work. Some people find that watching an engaging film provides mental rest in a way that watching anything that happens to be on TV doesn't. How about reading or listening to an interesting book or podcast for 15 minutes, doing a puzzle or helping your kids with their Lego? These all count as mental rest, providing you can engage with them fully and not get distracted into your old thinking patterns. You could have a go at learning a new physical skill, sport or anything else that engages the brain in a totally different way. Engaging in something that's physically challenging and immerses you in an intense experience is akin to meditation because you're forcing yourself to concentrate mentally as well as exercise yourself physically. We recommend this because it stops you from drifting off into your usual thinking patterns.

Sensory rest

In a world where there's no end to the amount of stimulation you can experience, shutting off your senses can be tricky. But it's a type of rest all humans need to some extent. Powering down your technology for a while is intended to provide you with a sensory rest and this can be helpful. Providing yourself with deliberate periods of sensory deprivation is one way to achieve sensory rest but there are many other ways to do it. For example, visual rest can include looking at nature or even the wallpaper for 15 seconds or more in between pieces of work. If you look down at your laptop or phone for work, try looking up when you take some visual rest, as it provides a natural shift in your usual physiology and can also lift your spirits. Auditory rest can include some quiet time away from sounds and distractions but can also include listening to music or even phoning a friend, providing these are things that you don't otherwise do all day. If you work in customer service, talking to customers all day then phoning a friend might be nice but won't provide you with sensory rest.

Creative rest

If you work in a creative space, you'll occasionally need some creative rest. Some people need creative rest because their natural thinking patterns mean that they're programmed to do something with every creative opportunity. This is a brilliant skill to have but if it becomes compulsive it can be counterproductive, not to mention exhausting. Taking creative rest involves experiencing the world without feeling the compulsion to do something with what you observe. Try going for a walk without taking the camera or reading a book just for fun.

Start small and stay aware

We believe small changes can make a huge difference to your mental capacity, your ability to think clearly and make good decisions. It's normal to see this as yet another thing to do, so it works best if you can build something naturally into your routine and that of your team. They can and preferably should be simple things rather than elaborate or time-consuming things. Set an alarm every few hours to walk away from your laptop for 15 minutes and do something physical, even if it's putting on some washing (if you're working from home) or making a cup of tea. We suggest looking at your diary and considering where there might be scope for some mental rest, whether it's reading a paper over lunch, listening to some music, wandering around a gallery or having a conversation with a friend. Be aware of when and where you act compulsively and avoid mental rest but convince yourself it's a good thing. Typical patterns to watch out for are working long hours, particularly if it impedes your sleep, or leaving your phone on overnight or during times when it would be appropriate to turn it off. Very few people have a job where someone will literally die if they don't respond immediately to a message, so unless you work in the emergency services and are on call, power down and don't fall for your own excuses.

Consider building the opportunity for mental rest into your organisational working patterns. You could decide to hold online meetings between 11 am and 3 pm, leaving the rest of the day free from in-person or video calls. You can also provide mental rest as part of work by restricting the medium for communication and engagement. An increasing number of organisations are trialling the four-day week, providing an opportunity for maximum respite where everyone in the organisation switches off.

Ways that organisations can provide mental rest

Organisations that take mental rest seriously use their environment to provide mental rest by having 'no technology' zones. One we work with has a library with physical books, comfy seating and a rule of silence so that people can come for mental rest. They also have a rule that technology must be locked in safes during off-site meetings. A firm of architects has a coffee area where people can come and talk without their technology and be inspired by models and photos of great architecture.

The project lead of a creative design organisation specifies the medium of choice for each meeting. One meeting may be whiteboard only, one might use sticky notes, one may be purely discussion with no notetaking. This minimises sensory distractions and provides both mental rest and focus. Not everyone likes rules but if these zones are created with the involvement of employees they usually work well.

Key takeaways

⊠ Mental rest is essential in today's overstim-
ulating world, even more so if you're prone
to overthinking or you're a creative thinker.
However, people aren't always good at
exercising discipline as the pull of work or
technology can be addictive.

⊠ If you're able to build ways for people to
have mental rest in their day-to-day work,
it will be much easier to achieve and will
support them in maintaining a sustainable
routine.

⊠ You also need your own personalised
strategies, enabling you to become a good
role model for your team and colleagues.

⊠ Taking action to ensure mental rest will help
you and your team avoid mental exhaustion
as well as keeping a clear head for when it's
needed, which is critical for performance.

Chapter 4
Emotional rest

Emotional exhaustion is a core component of burnout. It was originally identified in people working in caring roles, such as counsellors, therapists, social care workers and front-line medical workers. However, the changing nature of the role of leaders in organisations and the increasing expectations of them from employees, regulators and society more generally has increased their emotional burden. This is also the reality for other roles, including managers and HR professionals. Consequently these roles now fit into a high-risk category in terms of emotional exhaustion. If your work involves some kind of emotional engagement, then we suggest you have a think about what constitutes emotional rest and design it into your work practice.

Today's leaders and managers are responsible for much more than organising work to meet a strategy. These roles have pastoral and caring elements that are increasingly critical to employee health and seen as part of being a responsible employer. Responsibilities for monitoring team mental health, implementing strategies to support diversity and inclusion as well as coaching and developing team members are all attributes of good leadership. However, they also increase emotional load. This is especially true for leaders and managers who care deeply about their work and their teams.

HR professionals also typically carry a heavy emotional burden. Their work frequently involves being privy to sensitive and sometimes uncomfortable information that they're unable to share for confidentiality reasons. HR teams must also deal with all the areas that are tough when it comes to being an employer, involving topics that deeply affect people's lives – for example, dealing with grievances, performance problems, team conflicts and employee health issues. All of this can subject HR professionals to the kind of intense emotional exposure that their professional training doesn't provide them with the skills to handle. They have the technical training to handle the legal and professional processes involved but not the training that's required to process the emotional impact of this work. When you add to this the fact that most people don't understand what's required in leadership, management and HR roles and that they're often underappreciated and criticised, it's no wonder that levels of burnout are particularly high in this population.

Emotional overload mostly comes from working intensely with other people but can also happen if you're emotionally invested in your work. This is common in creative roles where people are heavily invested in their creative process and the outcome of the work. A lot of emotional toil will leave you exhausted and if you don't build in space for emotional rest, you'll also be at risk of burnout. Included in this bracket are people working on scientific endeavours and in any innovative industry, though there are many roles, creative and otherwise, that people are heavily emotionally invested in where there's a need for emotional rest. Even in seemingly normal professional roles, people who care about getting it right are at risk of emotional exhaustion. Whether you're preparing a set of accounts or packing up a delivery, we'd suggest that if you're emotionally invested, you're at risk of emotional exhaustion. Of course, the challenge for organisations is that they want people to care about their work and emotionally invested people are more diligent, loyal and motivated. But this comes with negative side effects. If organisations don't encourage people to take emotional rest, staff turnover will increase, morale will suffer and performance will be negatively impacted as people become so emotionally tired that they become apathetic and despondent.

Consider the roles within your organisation that are generally emotionally draining or where, at specific times, there's an increase in emotional burden. Examples of the latter include during redundancies, organisational changes or intense or important projects. What kind of emotional burden are you personally subjected to, either in your day-to-day work or in specific organisational challenges? Leaders are only human. Sucking it up and pushing through may work for a while but eventually it will take its toll. We recommend taking the time to ensure you've built in the appropriate amount of emotional rest as part of your own rhythm and that of your organisation. Failing to do this will have a significant long-term impact on your health and the health of your employees as well as the ongoing success of the organisation.

Emotional rest is about having a break from the work that most engages and uses up your emotional energy. Whereas mental rest can be achieved in short bursts of time, emotional rest usually needs longer time spans to enable your emotions to regulate and stabilise. By now, you'll have realised that emotional rest doesn't mean a bit of downtime before your next meeting or a day off after an intense few weeks of emotionally draining activity. Given this longer time span, a bit more thought and planning is required.

Consider where you have chunks of time available that will enable you to do this well. Can you organise your emotionally draining work into a few days a week, giving you time to do other work on other days? This can be an effective strategy for a lot of people. If you spread this kind of work throughout the week, you don't give yourself enough time to recover before going back to it; many people find that doing emotionally demanding work intensively, then taking a block of time away from it, is helpful. In the emergency services, shift work is planned in this way so that first responders are in an intense mindset for their work, followed by extended time to recover and recharge. That said, if your work involves regular periods of emotional strain or you have a particular circumstance that has created an intense period of emotional burden, longer periods of emotional rest may well be required.

Emotional rest includes thinking about what social rest you need. You may feel energised by being with other people but everyone needs to take a break from social pressures. This is particularly the case for those who work in roles that have a high level of connection with other people or those who would normally invest a lot in their personal relationships. Here are some practical suggestions to get you started.

Organise your time for emotional respite

If it's practically possible, organise yourself so that you can take longer breaks away from emotionally intensive work. This is even more essential if you're also expected to perform while doing this type of work. We appreciate that this can be challenging but with a bit of creativity and flexibility it should be possible. Think about the work you do that isn't emotionally intense. Can you block that together in days or half days of work? Everyone has aspects of their work that are less emotionally intense, including administrative tasks or straightforward meetings. These may not be fun but they don't need to be – they just need to give you a break from the emotionally draining work. Here are a few real life examples to get you thinking about what might work best for you.

Using creativity for emotional rest

Beth is a successful executive coach who gets her emotional rest by doing creative things. She engages in creative activities such as photography, baking and playing music. This works well for her because she finds that if she sits around, she starts to worry about her clients and that engages her emotions back into work. She likes to work intensively because it's a good rhythm for her but she takes long periods of time off so that she can recharge properly and disconnect from the inevitable absorption of other people's problems. These are planned well in advance to avoid issues for her clients.

Providing emotional rest for the team

Mabel is the leader of a large team of project managers who are involved in resolving a lot of project-related issues, particularly team conflicts and stresses. This leaves her team feeling the burden of being the 'fixers' and causing them to become emotionally drained. Mabel has weekly open-door sessions where her team can discuss what's happening on their projects. She provides coaching and support but mainly listens. She knows they know how to fix things; they just need to talk it out. This relieves their emotional burden and, because she only does this for one day a week, Mabel can take an emotional rest for the remainder of the week.

She uses her manager and coach to reflect on everything she's heard, which helps her to spot themes and identify specific actions that can be taken as well as unburden her own concerns at the same time.

Groups can emotionally recharge together

This can be particularly powerful if the group experiences similar emotionally intense pressures, for example leadership groups or HR professionals. Debriefing as a group, sharing experiences and decompressing together are great ways of combining emotional rest with much-needed social support. In an innovative product organisation, the HR professionals organise team retreats after emotionally exhausting pieces of work. They spend the first day debriefing the work as a group; the second day in full retreat mode, spending time together or alone based on personal preference; and the third day reflecting on lessons learned and planning. This gives them much needed emotional rest but also a way of emotionally processing their work and taking away learning ready for re-engagement into the workplace and the practise phase.

Build in time for a debrief

To get effective emotional rest you need time away from emotionally demanding work and a mechanism for working the emotion out of your system. People who work in highly emotionally charged environments tend to take on other people's emotions, largely because when someone experiences empathy they naturally connect with the other person's emotional state, therefore experiencing a little of it themselves. This is completely normal; to a greater or lesser extent and depending on their personality, people do this every day. However, if your job means that you're experiencing it at an increased intensity and with increased frequency, you'll naturally become more emotionally overloaded over time. To remedy this, you need to find ways to process the build-up of emotion as well as time away from the cause of it. In clinical settings, people doing emotionally intense work undertake what's known as supervision. Rather than a management function, it's simply a way to share your work and experience with a more experienced professional. This person can provide a more objective perspective, provide guidance or advice or simply listen and understand.

Organisations whose people engage in emotionally intense work are now providing more opportunities for them to debrief in a similar way with a coach, a mentor or a peer support group. If you don't already do this or it's something that happens on an ad hoc basis, consider building it into your own and your team's rhythm. While it will be an important process after particularly intense periods, building it into the normal organisational rhythm will help to avoid a build-up of emotional burden and reduce the likelihood of you or your team burning out. This means structuring it with a regular cadence into how you do your work.

As a leader, designing a rhythm for emotional rest needs to fit with your own personality and style. You may find that practising your own form of spirituality helps. Alternatively, you may find that spending some time alone, and some with family or friends, is beneficial. Gentle exercise works well for a lot of people but you need to be mindfully engaged in the exercise, not just walking while thinking about your work. Walking in the countryside or along a beach works well for many as this provides a different view to engage your mind as well as some gentle physical exercise. Intensive exercise such as running or cardio works less well for processing emotion. These forms of exercise are designed to put your body under pressure, which is good for building physical capabilities but not so good for processing emotions as the exercise will only add to the build-up of cortisol in your body. Therefore during periods of emotional rest we suggest easing off on the triathlon training.

Different perspectives also support emotional rest. A change in visual perspective, such as the view from the top of a hill or down a long beach, is a good way to do this. You can also engage in something completely different. A life coach we work with gets emotional rest by helping out at a women's refuge. While this might look like replacing one emotionally intense experience for another, she says that when doing work at the refuge she feels she's making a practical difference and it frees her up emotionally. She doesn't work for them as a coach. What works for you will depend on how you process your emotions, so it's worth trying a few things and noticing whether you feel lighter afterwards. If the answer is yes, keep going.

Key takeaways

¤ Emotional rest is something we all need from time to time. How much depends largely on the work you do, its level of emotional intensity and your own personal style.

¤ An increasing number of organisational roles carry a disproportionate amount of emotional burden. This includes leaders, managers and HR professionals.

¤ By equipping people with the knowledge they need to take emotional rest and planning emotional rest into your organisational rhythm, you'll build resilience in both team and organisation so that everyone will be in the right place emotionally when it comes to the perform phase.

Chapter 5
The practise phase

In our experience organisations don't practise enough. Organisations don't perform, nor do they need to perform, every minute of every day. They need to be able to perform at different times during a day, week, month or year. They may need to increase effort and focus for key projects or seasonal events and deal with critical issues as they arise. Performance is required for the achievement of outcomes and the management of key pressure points. These happen less frequently than some like to admit. We find that in many organisations, there's a compulsion to be busy all the time. Doing more and more activities and performing at an impossible '110 per cent' all the time is an addiction that we believe is both unnecessary and unrealistic. There's no denying that many people work hard, feel under pressure and seem to have more to do than hours in the day. However, we believe that this hard work is frequently caused by a lack of practice rather than a drive for performance.

Organisations frequently expend a lot of energy at the start of a project or when they need to get something 'over the line' and can galvanise themselves in a crisis but don't keep themselves fit enough to see things through. This is because they don't have the right processes in place to practise effectively. Organisational leaders often don't place enough value on the practise phase and launch into a new activity with the belief that laborious effort is what makes something successful, when in fact the effort becomes a necessity because the practise phase has been ignored. You may well disagree with this and be able to provide example after example of successful projects achieved without such a phase. While we appreciate that may be the case, the question we're asking here is was all that effort absolutely necessary? Could the same outcome have been achieved more easily, more quickly or more efficiently? If you were to study the progress of such projects closely, you'd be likely to find examples of delays and frustration caused by a lack of sufficient planning and set-up, a lack of a clear objective, a lack of the required skills for certain tasks and poor communication channels. We suggest that a commitment to practising effectively would resolve many of these problems.

Sports have had this down for a long time. This may be because so much of sporting performance is connected to the condition of the sports professional's body and the importance of keeping it in shape is both understood and valued. Sports professionals also understand that elite performance doesn't come from heroic effort. They understand the value of practising skills and techniques to help them perform at their best.

From that focus and understanding, sports have taken the concept of the practise phase to the next level, with incredible results. In the past five to ten years there has been an increasing emphasis on general conditioning as well as technical training for sportspeople. The men's England football team does Pilates, F1 drivers do cardio workouts to counteract the intense punishment the body experiences during a race and tennis players do strength training to help them to stay injury free and play for longer. In elite sports it's widely understood that there are periods where you perform at your peak and times for building muscle memory and habits that allow you to perform at your peak when you need to. The ability and confidence to perform over time and when you need to can only be developed in the practise phase.

Either before a match or on days when they're not due to play, tennis players practise. They practise techniques for a particular opponent, building muscle memory in the process so it comes out naturally in the game itself. They practise for certain conditions, often arriving in a country well in advance of a tournament to acclimatise. Most professional tennis players train for about four to five hours a day, which is high when you consider the amount of time they spend playing competitive matches (on average between 90 minutes and three hours). Tennis players practise for key moments in a match such as set points or serves where they need to be calm under pressure. They know they can't simply turn up and through effort alone expect to be successful. They practise knowing that this can tip the scales in their favour in a match. F1 specifically builds practice sessions into race weekends. These sessions enable the drivers and technicians to become familiar with track conditions, test new strategies and build confidence to perform in the race itself. Even the most experienced sports professionals don't just turn up and expect to perform well.

There appears to be a common belief in organisations that the practise phase isn't necessary. When a business hires someone with a core skill or expertise, the expectation is that they should be able to perform straight away and consistently all day, every day. As a leader, think about that for yourself and your team. Does that make sense? If elite sportspeople, the best in their field, practise regularly, day after day, when they're already at the top of their game, why do leaders in organisations expect themselves and their teams to perform at a consistently high level without practice?

We believe that minimal consideration is given to what it means and what's needed for people to perform well in their role within a particular project or more generally within the organisation. This lack of consideration and absence of the practise phase results in organisations having to redo work, backtrack on projects and decisions, rectify mistakes and put out fires that could have been avoided. Skipping the practise phase may feel more productive in the moment but it costs dearly in the long run. Think back to a project or piece of work that didn't go well. What were the failure points? What could you have done to avoid these? Would it have been useful to take the time to practise the skills, coordination and teamwork necessary to be successful?

We think that there are some common points of failure that could be mitigated, if not avoided completely, by some form of practise phase. Common failure points include getting into action too soon without a coordinated plan, communication issues, lack of clarity around decision making, too little or too much time reporting progress, leadership problems, egos and politics getting in the way and not practising for a crisis. Notice that these are all issues created by people, not ideas, processes or policies. You may have a beautiful Gantt chart but that doesn't mean people will follow it.

What does your organisation need to practise to make sure it's fit and ready for what it needs to do? Do you regularly practise together to handle difficult situations? This doesn't mean a once a year training or team awayday. Groups within organisations commonly don't spend enough time working together and practising cooperation to ensure they perform at the highest level when it's essential. Effective collaboration doesn't happen by accident. This is particularly true at a senior level where people are time poor and often feel they're spread too thinly. When senior leadership teams get together, all too often they end up in reporting mode, sharing information or advising on what they're doing or will be doing. Sadly, they rarely work together. It's almost as if, once you get to a senior level, you must be so good at all the communication stuff that you can build trust and work together without any practice at all. This doesn't ring true. The people side of leadership is without doubt the hardest part and senior leadership teams could save a lot of time and energy by taking time to work together more often.

Organisations that do the practise phase well know that the performance window is a small but critical one.

Emergency services practise for every eventuality or disaster so that when it happens, they have the process in their muscle to act quickly and decisively. Surgeons have limited days in surgery and spend a lot of time preparing the patient, the team and themselves so that the surgery is a success.

A colleague of ours leads the crisis planning team for a county council in England. This small team of people spend most of their time either planning drills, doing drills or debriefing on drills. This builds confidence in the team that they'll be able to perform when they need to.

These examples stand out because they involve risk to life but represent an exemplar of performance from outside the world of sport. We believe they're worthy comparisons. Sadly, though, most organisations don't prioritise the type of practice that would allow them to perform well when they need to and therefore when they do perform the whole activity is harder, less efficient and more stressful than it needs to be.

It's common for a lot of larger organisations to subcontract the practise phase to their learning and development teams or, in smaller organisations, the only HR person. These teams (and individuals) have the thankless task of trying to find solutions for the whole organisation. They often try desperately to engage leaders who are too busy (supposedly) performing but what they're really doing is cleaning up the mess that wouldn't have been created if they'd practised more.

These people end up feeling disconnected from the business and making training and learning decisions based on a best guess. They then spend too much of their time pushing water up a hill, trying to convince senior leaders of the need for learning and development activities. They're often met with the response that everyone is too busy getting on with the real work to spend time on learning. We suggest that's the wrong way round: people are too busy because they haven't spent time in the practise phase.

The good news is that with a little thought, planning and commitment, we believe organisations can easily make considerable improvements to their practise phase. This part of the book will provide you with some practical suggestions about how to go about this and suggest ways to design a practise phase that makes sense for your organisation and improves overall performance. The following chapters will explore how you can practise for improvement, practise new things and practise correcting errors. First, though, here are some general considerations for the design of the practise phase that are applicable to most organisations.

Relationship building

If your performance depends on teamwork or even basic levels of coordination between people, relationship building will be critical in the practise phase. People who understand each other create an effective shorthand that makes communication in the perform phase highly efficient. Colleagues who have spent time getting to know each other in this phase will need to speak to or check in with each other less frequently in the performance window because they can confidently predict how others will see and value things. A group that understands each other is also less likely to have major conflicts and those that arise are quickly resolved with minimum fuss. And the icing on the cake is that with the right amount of team building, people are less likely to feel threatened by each other, so you'll see less political game playing and land grabbing. What's not to like?

The problem often cited with relationship building is that it takes too long and some of the methods of doing so don't work well. We agree that this is a fair comment. Simply getting people together won't automatically build relationships and when people do bring in external facilitators to help the process along, they're not always a good match for the group or adequately skilled in the nuances of group dynamics and psychology. If you want to build relationships in a group effectively you need to make time to do it and you may need external professional help. Overall, what you need to do is plan it well. We observe that a common problem organisations experience is that in their desire for efficiency and cost effectiveness, they try to fit all their team building into a one-day event and cram in lots of other things such as strategy discussions and action plans at the same time. This is apparently known as 'making the most of it'. It's baffling that people expect to get value out of these types of days but they've become an accepted part of business. HR professionals are often unwilling to question such demands as something is better than nothing and facilitators are often too scared to challenge them as it may cost them a day's work. This approach is understandable from the point of view of everyone involved but ultimately it's ineffective and not the best use of precious resources in terms of time and money.

We believe that the best way to build relationships is to do it regularly over time and in shortish bursts that are focused only on this outcome and nothing else. A pattern that works well could be three half days, spaced over a few months, with team social time after each session. This isn't a significant investment for any group, allowing time in between to practise and build on the work done at each half day, which will make a significant difference to the overall result.

Whether you're using an internal or external facilitator, factor in the personalities of your team before choosing the person for that role. Engage in the process of finding the person with the right skills and experience. Don't just expect your learning and development (L&D) team to provide someone. If you have a high energy, extroverted team then icebreakers and team games may work well. If you have a team of serious-minded engineers or scientists, someone who can facilitate reflections and grounded discussions would be more appropriate. These types of people will explode if you ask them to wear a silly hat! While extroverted facilitators may argue that these 'fun' games will help bring people out of themselves, they're frequently viewed as shaming and only result in people shutting down. People who are more introverted will just feel threatened and this isn't conducive to building trust and psychological safety in a group. For some of you, it will be important for a facilitator to have knowledge of your industry or area of performance. While a lot of external facilitators have broad experience across different industries, if you work in a sector that's highly technical or there's a lot of shorthand, having someone who understands this will be a significant help. With a little focus and forethought, you can design highly effective ways of building relationships in your team without it taking up huge chunks of time.

Training and development

If your L&D offering isn't working for your business it's probably too general and not focused on the key skills, capabilities and areas of self-development that you need to ensure performance in your organisation. Don't blame your L&D team for this: they aren't mind readers – they need your help. As a leader, think about what skills, capabilities and personal attributes you need in your organisation to be able to perform and focus on those. When thinking about training and development in a rest, practise, perform mindset, it's not always the obvious things that are the biggest levers for performance. Many organisational programmes include technical skills training and maybe management capabilities and leadership development but what specifically do you need in each of those elements? And what essentials are you missing that could make the difference when it comes to performance?

Focus on the skills that are essential for performance

Riva is the L&D lead for a biotech organisation working on cures for cancer. Much of the organisation is made up of scientists or academics. While thinking about leadership and management development, Riva's challenge was that these technically brilliant people really struggled to collaborate effectively but she found it hard to get them engaged enough to go on a development programme. Additionally, the programmes on offer in the market were generalised. She didn't need them to think commercially, give great feedback or even create a compelling vision; they just needed to be excellent at collaboration. She decided these skills needed to be developed in the real world of their work so instead she set up a coaching programme where they could get one-to-one bespoke support. She hired coaches with biotech experience so they could build rapport quickly and establish credibility with the scientists. These coaches also attended some of the group meetings so they could work with the whole team on collaboration skills and nothing else. It provided focused skills development with minimal time commitment.

If it's important for your people to perform under pressure or make clear decisions quickly, they need to be emotionally regulated. If your people are working on life-changing technology or in intense client-facing situations, they probably need to develop more resilience than most people. Can your people work with the appropriate level of perspective, remain calm under pressure and be able to separate out noise, emotion and overreaction from the key elements that need to be attended to? Are you and your team practised at being able to handle the pressure of what it takes to perform at certain times? These needs are complex and the solutions will be unique to each individual. Therefore they're best met through one-to-one work rather than generalised group training.

Coaching

Sportspeople appreciate the importance of coaching and a coaching approach. In elite sports, everyone has at least one coach and each one focuses on a different aspect of what's required to perform at the highest level. Some coaching is technical and some is more focused on mindset. In tennis and F1 it's common for elite athletes to employ a technical coach, a mental or performance coach and a physical fitness coach of some kind. This is now becoming more common in football, although traditionally the team coach took on responsibility for all of it and for the whole team, which is quite an endeavour.

There is an increasing number of robust studies highlighting the return on investment to organisations who invest in coaching, which is reported to be between an impressive 500 and 650 per cent (Cartwright & Cooper 2009). Coaching is also widely considered to be an effective way of transferring training material into practice following the attendance of training programmes as it facilitates the behavioural changes required to accompany the knowledge and learning. One study found that coaching and training combined resulted in an 88 per cent increase in performance compared to 22 per cent for training alone (Cartwright & Cooper 2009). As coaching is an unregulated industry, research shows a wide range of effectiveness depending on the quality of the coach and therefore organisations must ensure they employ coaches who are suitably qualified and experienced.

Mentoring and on-the-job learning

Think about which aspects of training and development are best done in day-to-day work. You may decide that leaders and managers need to prioritise time to help people learn on the job rather than formally. Peer-to-peer learning is also becoming increasingly popular and can be effective but it's fraught with issues from the perspective of the practise phase. Peer-to-peer learning is informal and based on people coming forward as volunteers to teach others. This is great if the people involved are exemplars of a particular skill but if they're simply enthusiastic amateurs, you could end up inadvertently spreading errors throughout the organisation. The reality is that for most organisations, their best performers are often perceived as being too busy performing to teach others. When you consider the organisation's overall performance, this could be counterproductive. Freeing up your best performers to conduct training on specific and critical skills and mentoring others will pay huge dividends during the perform phase.

Focusing on the hygiene factors of running an organisation effectively during the practise phase is a worthwhile investment. Attending to hygiene factors means working on getting the basics right, as without them the organisation will start to crumble under pressure. For example, it's frightening to think about the amount of time that's wasted on badly run meetings. If you work on making sure even routine meetings are well run, facilitated skilfully and with clear follow-through, you'll be in better shape to perform when you need to.

The following chapters will focus on specific areas of the practise phase: improvement, developing something new and correcting errors.

Key takeaways

¤ Rethink how you practise in your organisation. Start with what you need for
performance and work back from there.

¤ Invest time and budgets in the areas that
are complex and require expertise.

¤ Where it will be the most helpful, find
ways to build in learning on the job and
think about where investing in relationship building will provide you with a strong
foundation.

Chapter 6
Practise for improvement

What do you need to do to improve performance? Is it communication? Is it skills? Is it team dynamics? Is it processes or decision making? These and many other aspects of organisational life can almost always be improved upon but will it help your performance? As a leader, you may normally identify improvement areas through what has gone wrong in a particular project or area of the organisation. However, the focus of this chapter is on improving what is already working to make it better and more efficient. This will help you to build on the performance you already have.

Just because you can always improve doesn't mean you should. The Japanese term *kaizen* has become popular and is now commonly used by consultancies and in organisations. When translated, it means 'improvement' and was born out of the success of the Japanese car building industry. Countless models and processes claiming to be kaizen can be found in management consultancy PowerPoint decks and strategic development books. This must be a good thing, right? Well, maybe, but we believe the term has created issues for organisations and the people in them who apply the principle too broadly, believing everything must be continually improved. Having a kaizen mindset shows you're dedicated to getting better and improving yourself but when it comes to organisations you need to be careful which parts of the company you assign the kaizen approach to.

If you're a fan or follower of the kaizen approach, you'll know that one of the key elements is that the improvement is focused on the key areas that lead to performance. It's systemic in that it considers the whole system and finds ways to improve it that have a substantial impact on the overall performance of the organisation. Kaizen was revolutionary when it was first introduced because it included the people elements of an organisation as well as management principles, leadership and ways of communicating that weren't directly related to the technical aspects of work. This seems obvious now but when it was developed after the Second World War, it was groundbreaking for organisations to consider performance through this lens. However, what's often missed in the way kaizen is applied today is that it takes careful analysis and practice to identify what the key elements are.

If you apply continual improvement too broadly without identifying which are the key areas that will provide you with the biggest payoff in terms of performance, you're wasting a lot of time and resources. People who feel under pressure with too much to do and insufficient resources often have an issue with prioritisation. If you have lots of equal priorities, then you have none. Priorities should always be stack ranked: one is always more important than the other, otherwise it's not a priority.

When it comes to improvement projects or initiatives, it's best to think through how the improvement you're suggesting will help you perform better in terms of your organisational outcomes. As a leader, you may need to be critical of yourself because there are many ways in which to argue that an idea or activity will contribute to performance. While that may be true, how much will it impact performance? Are you focusing on what's easier to deliver rather than what's necessary and what's politically acceptable rather than what needs to be done? When considering improvement, ask yourself or others why this is important. What's the outcome of this activity? What will this initiative deliver in terms of performance? All too often we find that improvement projects are undertaken because they're popular, big and shiny, or a senior leader's pet idea. Ideally, only initiatives that will give you a measurable and sustainable return should be pursued.

At the risk of upsetting high achievers, good enough is often good enough. Some aspects of organisational work just need to be OK. Doing them better will add little or nothing to the overall performance of the organisation. That said, you may still decide to work on some of these things if they have a positive impact on morale, they're part of the organisational culture or it's your favourite idea. There's nothing wrong with that, provided you're honest with yourself as to why you're doing it and not justifying it through some tenuous link to performance.

In F1, where small increments can make the difference between pole position and being at the back of the grid, teams practise with different technical settings, tyre combinations and strategies. It's not all down to driver performance or just about whether the car is good. A whole team of engineers work on making minute incremental adjustments to get the best out of the car and driver. The pit crew regularly practise pit stops to avoid mistakes and improve by tiny margins the time the car spends in the pits. In tennis, serving an ace can be a game changer. It preserves energy otherwise spent in long rallies (however entertaining that may be for spectators) and renders your opponent helpless. It's no wonder players spend a lot of time practising their serve and players with a strong service game tend to do well in big tournaments. In both sporting examples, the resources of time, energy and money are allocated to improvements where they really count. Let's look at some specific considerations when thinking about practising for improvement in organisations.

Be clear on the time and resources you have available

Many things can be improved; the question is what *should* be improved? One of the key considerations in answering that question is this: how much time and resources are available? This will help you prioritise your improvement activity. This is a question both in absolute terms of available time and resources and relative terms, ie where to spend the available time and resources to maximise the positive impact on overall performance. It can be tempting to spread your time and resources too thinly, commonly known as 'peanut buttering'. This is usually a waste of time and resources as nothing is given the focus it deserves. We appreciate that decisions to 'peanut butter' come from good intentions. Leaders want to be seen as fair and reasonable and if this is your reason for thinly spreading time and resources then that's OK. Just don't expect it to have an impact on performance. To make an impact with improvement, resources need to be focused and committed.

Look beyond the obvious

We find that in organisations, the key areas of the practise phase aren't always immediately obvious. Humans spend a lot of time and energy working around things rather than taking the time to do or learn things that will save them time and effort later. The human need for instant gratification means that people don't invest time and energy to create sustainable solutions. Instead, they look for quick and easy wins. This is particularly the case with activities that aren't interesting or particularly exciting. Organisations often focus on the obvious, the shiny or the physical. They don't think through the less obvious components that make a big difference but are less easy to measure or don't provide instant gratification. Examples of this include personal development areas such as leadership, time management and planning skills, as well as organisational issues such as clearer processes, better decision making, effective communication and ceasing activities. Organisations frequently struggle to get their employees engaged with technology, even when it's obvious it will bring them benefits. As a leader, do you grind it out through hard work so that you get through it but everyone leaves exhausted? Instead, we recommend looking at what created the 'too much effort' mindset and focusing on improving that. Once you've identified the areas of improvement that will boost performance, plan and protect time and resources to practise them.

Invest in your people

If the main factor impacting performance is your people, then we believe you must invest in leadership and management capabilities. In people-centric organisations, your ability to plan and organise other people will be a key contributing factor to the performance or otherwise of your organisation. Organisations usually employ different structural strategies to achieve this, including taking out management layers, creating self-managing teams and matrix systems. These and other strategies are an attempt to create a nimbler way of organising, move away from a creativity-draining command and control culture and ultimately improve performance. The way you organise your people also depends on your outcome, whether in the organisation as a whole, a particular team or a project.

Whatever the organisational structure, you need well-developed leaders and managers to implement outcomes and make the most of the structure and expertise of your team. Organisations that have multidisciplinary teams will need strong leadership to coordinate, counsel and provide direction to a group of people who have individual expertise and need to work in a complementary rather than conflicting manner. We appreciate that this requires investment in leaders and managers in a way that will need to be more tailored than you might first think. Buying an off-the-shelf management programme may be less expensive but it may not give you what you need. We recommend thinking through your organisation's ways of working from a people perspective and considering what's needed when it comes to developing leadership and management capabilities. For example, in a flat structure, development reviews could be a straightforward process but, in an organisation where ambitious people are always looking at promotion, your managers will need the appropriate skills to manage this.

Practise during regular events and activities

All too often, we find that organisations try to learn how to do what's necessary in a pressurised situation where they need to perform. Teams naturally pull together during a crisis or when there's an exciting new project that a wide range of people from across the organisation want to get involved in. We suggest that these are the wrong times to practise. It's better to do it when there's less pressure.

How can you use your normal activities to improve the skills you'll need when the heat is on? It starts by identifying what you believe will, if improved, have a positive impact on performance. This is often in the areas of communication, team dynamics, decision making and setting clear goals. Using these examples, ahead of meetings you could practise being clearer about the goals of the meeting and encourage others to do the same. Try to avoid turning up and seeing what it's about or expecting others to do the same. Be clear about why the meeting has been called, why people are in it and what action, decision or information will be required. In the meetings, practise being clearer in how you communicate and encourage others to do the same, practising the skills of asking questions or getting curious about what someone's trying to say. If you find that meetings often become a talking shop where nothing's decided, practise forcing the group to make a decision. If people don't challenge each other at all in meetings or challenge in a negative or disruptive way, it's a good idea to practise how to challenge more effectively or respectfully.

As a leader, consider whether you need to make improvements in information-sharing processes rather than relying on meetings or emails. If too many people are invited to meetings for fear of upsetting someone or simply fear of missing out, practise consciously deciding who is invited to meetings and why. Only invite the people who need to be there. If everyone plus the organisation's cat is copied into an email 'for context' then practise reducing the number of people in the loop. While these and many other apparently trivial organisational behaviours may not immediately seem important to improve, you need to get them right in the day-to-day to stand any chance of them working in the performance window. Consider how these behaviours can limit or negatively impact the ability of an individual or team to perform at their best in a time of crisis, important time-bound projects or for urgent opportunities. Practising good behavioural and cultural habits can have a significant positive impact on performance when it's needed the most.

Improving communication in a growing organisation

As a senior leader in a growing manufacturing organisation, Alex realised that the informal method of communicating decisions and other important information was out of date. Rather than putting a formal structure in place, which is a common reaction to this challenge, Alex set about trying to understand the needs of the organisation. This enabled him to make improvements in the right places rather than initiate big, time-consuming projects. The main problem was that decisions took too long to reach the people who needed to know about them, leading to a confused and demoralised workforce. A lot of this was down to miscommunication in the senior leadership team, with some leaders assuming others would do it or even some confusion as to whether they'd even made a decision. Alex started by improving the way in which the senior leadership team ran their meetings, made decisions and discussed communicating any resulting actions. This simple improvement had an immediate positive impact. If Alex had taken a blanket approach and implemented new processes and initiatives, he would've missed the opportunity to have a quick win and wasted a lot of valuable time and energy.

Find ways to measure your improvement

Have a clear way of measuring what the correct and appropriate level of improvement is for your team or organisation. The term 'world class' is often used as an excuse to apply a broad-brush approach to improvement. It's a well-intentioned aspiration but with no clear idea as to what it means and why it's needed. Not everything needs to be world class. Egos and status-seeking can lead people in organisations to spend significant time and effort in talking up their area and its importance to either a project or organisation. While understandable from a human nature perspective, this can lead to an unnecessary amount of time and energy being spent on improvements that add little to the overall performance. Alternatively, some people's style means that they'll always look for the positive in anything – saying, for example, 'At least they've improved.' But the real question is, is it good enough for what you're seeking to do and has it, in fact, improved performance?

You can use a mixture of quantitative and qualitative measures. Intangible measurements provide a helpful guide for improvement, especially in organisations where there's less of a clear measurable output or the value of the output only becomes clear over a long period of time. These could include focus group outputs, contributions to suggestion boxes or insights from your peers. Unless it clearly illustrates what you're trying to measure, avoid an over-reliance on numerical data. These types of measures are often chosen because they appear more concrete but many crazy decisions are made on the back of numbers that were squeezed to fit a measurement. People's behaviour adapts to what gets measured in organisations, so be sure to choose measurements that encourage the behaviour you want to see.

When you're practising for improvement, expect to hit a plateau. You may feel like giving up at some point because improvements are coming in relatively small increments. At the beginning of learning anything new you'll make huge strides in improvement but this plateaus after a while. People who master skills work through this plateau and train themselves to notice the small improvements and think about incremental rather than big, showy improvements. So go easy on yourself and don't give up.

Key takeaways

⌗ The key to practising for improvement is to focus on the areas where improvement will boost your performance.

⌗ Avoid creating a culture where everyone is constantly trying to improve everything. This will induce change fatigue, waste time and resources and lower morale as people discover the microsite they've poured their heart and soul into has had no visitors.

⌗ If an area of the organisation is perfect for continual improvement cycles, set achievable improvement goals that are a stretch but doable and are measurable in some way.

⌗ Psychologically it's better to start small and build than to set huge targets and then have to scale back.

Chapter 7
Practise the new

Doing something new takes practice. Even a genius won't be able to do something new straight away and do it well. If someone can do something straight away, it probably isn't new. Despite this reality, leaders and organisations seem to act as if they or their teams can just pick something up with little or no practice, expecting people to 'work it out as they go along'. This may ultimately get some things done but, in our view, it's unlikely to lead to performance excellence. More likely, it will see people encode inefficiency and errors into the process and adopt workarounds in the pursuit of making it work. Aligned with this short-term approach to the new is to do a 'once and done' launch or training. People rarely 'get' something the first time and if the 'new' is important to the performance of the organisation, investing time in the practise phase becomes important. This is particularly true if the change relates to something people do infrequently. In such situations we suggest they'll need regular refreshers and reminders to develop and build their muscle memory.

Practising the new will vary in size and scope, from the relatively small – say, a new expenses system – through to new ways of working or a new appraisal process, all the way to major events such as a full-blown merger. Obviously, the practise phase will vary depending on what's new and the scale of what needs to be practised. Time dedicated to the practise phase should be based on the importance of the new thing as well as the size of the change. For example, while a new appraisal system may be a relatively small change for some organisations, if growing talent is a key aspect of performance, ensuring people are skilled in using it and all its features will be important. As this is likely to be a system that managers and leaders interact with only once or twice a year, refreshers and further training will be required to ensure they're sufficiently skilled to use the system properly.

Learning something new will take time and focus. If your team or organisation is working towards something that hasn't been done before, either in the organisation or the market, you need to think about the practise phase in terms of how to appropriately test and pilot the new thing. We appreciate that this isn't always easy to incorporate into a plan, particularly if the 'new' relates to projects, the deadlines are approaching and speed to market could make the difference between success and failure. The practise phase for anything new is what the leaders and programme managers we speak to have the most gripes about. People in these positions often understand the importance of the practise phase and start off with great intentions of building in sufficient time to practise. Inevitably, though, this good intention nearly always gets squeezed by demands for speed and urgency. Correspondingly, people in these positions also know that the lack of practice nearly always ends in more pain, time and effort in putting right the consequences of the squeeze. Even with this knowledge and repeated data to underline it, it remains an issue that organisations continually face. They don't practise and learn what's needed to improve performance in the future. They repeat this illusion of pace and speed rather than practise the skills to develop performance excellence. That said, we understand that you also need to be realistic. The real-world push for speed is a fact of organisational life. As a result, you'll need to think creatively about the practise phase to build in the requisite amount of time to avoid the main problems organisations often experience.

In a sport, the 'new' can occur when it undergoes a rule change or when a new manager or coach is appointed. One example of practising the new from a change of rules perspective is in F1. Every season, new car regulations provide an opportunity to go back to the drawing board. F1 teams spend a significant amount of time designing, building and testing a new car to meet the new regulations. The goal of this work is to meet the requirements of the new regulations while ensuring that they don't have an adverse impact on performance. Even then, despite all the attention to detail, a huge amount of adjustment to the car is made after the season starts and once the performance can be seen on the track. It's impossible to know for sure whether you have a good car until you start racing it and F1 teams use this feedback loop to practise and develop the car.

This is an important feedback loop for leaders in organisations as well. Unlike F1, leaders in business environments are often reluctant to pay attention to or act on the feedback they receive when implementing something new. This can be for several reasons, including pride, fear of criticism, fear of getting it wrong or a simple belief in the rightness of the decision despite evidence to the contrary. When improvements are still needed after the launch of something, this is often viewed as a failure rather than an extension of the practise phase. This is understandable as there can be a real risk to a leader's position if results don't go their way. That's why being clear about when the practise phase ends and the performance phase begins is essential to give yourself and those around you the confidence to experiment, practise and learn with the aim of improving performance.

In sport, it takes time to develop the muscle for a new style of play, a new team structure or to accommodate new developments in the sport itself. Leaders in sport know that and practise new formations, tactics and behaviours to reflect and incorporate this. They test them out in practice sessions, they pilot them in a match and they review and iterate in the post-match analysis, repeating the cycle of practice session, pilot and review. The goal is to understand how the 'new' has affected performance and what, if anything, is needed to improve it.

Organisations could and should do more of this but often don't. All too often, the 'new' is implemented and doubled down on as there's a belief that too much has been invested in it, whether that's resources or political capital. The opportunity cost is often seen as too high.

Practising the new requires the development of a culture that has the courage to maintain perspective and focus on the bigger picture.

Professional tennis players and football teams often watch hours of footage before playing new opponents, tracking their style, their strengths and the weaknesses that might be exploitable. In major tournaments, players and teams can't practise for every eventuality of the draw, so the practise phase against new opponents can be short. Players can then focus on practising the aspects of their game that are most likely to be successful against a particular opponent.

In practising the new, it's pragmatic to focus on what really matters before releasing it into the world, rather than trying to get everything perfect ahead of time. Notice that when practising the new, the approach is different from talking about how to improve performance, as in the previous chapter. When practising the new, your outcome is to avoid the main pitfalls and pain points. This might seem a bit negative at first glance. Surely it would be better to aim for boosting performance here too? In an ideal world, yes, but the reality of external pressures and a competitive landscape means that getting something perfect into the world is a rare thing indeed. Innovative sectors use this approach to increase their speed to market, continuing to iterate once a product is launched. In Silicon Valley there's even the mantra 'Move fast and break things'. It's debatable whether this is actually an optimal strategy but it's understandable in an industry that moves at breakneck speed. When thinking about what to test or pilot, consider the pitfalls you're trying to avoid and practise those thoroughly. Areas of lower impact or consequence can be addressed later.

Find a way to test out new ideas quickly

The unfamiliar makes human beings fearful and this is why the 'new' feels so risky. Therefore organisations can end up spending a lot of time trying to make an idea perfect before doing anything with it. The subsequent endless debates, revised documents and budget reviews usually result in something bland rather than something innovative. We've observed that innovative organisations turn this on its head. They choose ideas that are most likely to impact performance and find a way to test them out. Only after that do they revise and refine the idea. When identifying something to put to the test, we recommend designing a set of criteria whereby you can quickly assess whether this idea will impact performance and if it does, find a quick way to test or pilot it. It will feel less risky and give you useful feedback.

Develop a pilot

Using a pilot scheme enables organisations to test new initiatives in small, contained ways, get feedback and iterate. This saves time and resources as a pilot is less labour intensive and the organisation can position it as exploratory. This reduces the credibility risk to the leaders seeking to make the change. You can also focus the pilot to test specific elements of the 'new' to help stress test the key elements of the change or to incrementally introduce the new thing.

Spend time now to speed up later

Ben is a leader in an innovative product design organisation. He introduced a long experimentation cycle on new developments, often experimenting with multiple versions of a new product before deciding which to go to market with. This method builds the practise phase into the design phase, so that once a product is selected, the test and pilot phase is relatively short. Ben finds that it's more resource intensive upfront but saves time and energy later as several ideas have been robustly tested. Once the senior leadership team have chosen the product, it can get to market very quickly. Additionally, if something fails at the final hurdle, they can look back at previous work and easily pick up ideas and solutions.

Running a pilot in stages

Helen leads the L&D team at a medium-sized technology organisation that we work with. Her team uses pilots to test whether new programmes and initiatives deliver the level of behavioural change and related performance improvement that they want. They do this by testing the key elements of the initiative rather than trying to provide a state of the art training programme upfront. In highlighting the exploratory practise phase of the new initiative, everyone who attends knows it's a pilot and commits to giving detailed feedback on specific areas.

After the first pilot, based on feedback, more design work is done and then tested on a larger group with less detailed feedback. This is the 'go or no go' group. If the pilot is successful in delivering the behavioural change and desired performance improvement in this group, the programme is further refined and rolled out.

Iterating by using a pilot in this way helps the L&D team to be nimble. The fast and scrappy nature of the first pilot also means that no one involved feels overly invested in the design and therefore everyone's more open minded about change. This is an important factor as people can get too invested in an idea or initiative, which can lead an individual or group to stick with something that's ineffective. Helen is clear with her team (and herself) that discarded ideas are not a waste of time but part of the practise process. The programmes Helen designs are consistently well attended, get great feedback and wider buy-in as people working outside the L&D team feel involved in the design process.

Look to build on what's already there

Avoid the temptation to make a big statement by changing everything in a particular area or way of working. This is understandable, especially when someone comes into a new role or there's a lot of noise or hype around a particular topic. As a leader, you want to be seen to be doing something – and putting your stamp on a significant piece of work feels like a good way to do it. People also get excited about shiny new things or claim an idea is totally unique but lose out on valuable time by not considering what already exists. Tempting as it can be, if in the 'new' there's anything vaguely similar to what you're already doing, to save time and effort in the practise phase we suggest using what's already known or in existence. Modelling out what already works and building on it is efficient and can result in higher-quality outcomes. Nothing is completely new; learning frequently happens on the foundations of previous experience. When there's an issue, it's rarely the case that everything's wrong. When there's an opportunity, it's rarely the case that everything needs to be new. Given that, which elements of what you already have that you believe contribute to your performance do you want to maintain or even improve? It could be team dynamics, the acquisition and development of talent, attention to detail, the strength of the leadership team or past successes.

It's essential to be clear about the foundations of performance you're building your 'new' on. We appreciate that taking time to understand this may seem to some like looking backwards rather than forwards. Focus on modelling out what has worked well for you in the past and ensure that isn't lost when practising the new. What really contributed to your previous successful performance? Ensure that's retained in what's being created.

Building on best practice from other industries

Sarah works for a hotel chain that opened a new, high-end hotel just after the pandemic. Staff shortages meant that recruiting experienced hospitality professionals was tough and the hotel was still being finished due to the delays of lockdown. One of the key elements to the success of the business was the investment in training staff. Normally, following recruitment, the new team would be trained in situ for several weeks. However, as the building work continued with delays and events were already planned for the opening, Sarah had to think creatively. She knew that time to practise was critical. Ideally this time should be in the working environment but that wasn't possible. Instead of cutting short the practise phase she used a strategy commonly used by cruise ship companies that often train staff while the ship is being built. Instead of creating something new, she decided to utilise this proven method, which was new to her company. She set up a simulation in an unoccupied office building, creating an environment as close to the real thing as possible, and ran the training there. With four weeks of additional practice, the opening went without a hitch.

Key takeaways

- ¤ The reality when practising anything new is that you won't have the time you think you need.
- ¤ Hone your practise phase to test the genuinely new elements and focus on avoiding the biggest potential failures. This will help you shorten the practise phase while doing what's needed to launch high-quality innovations.
- ¤ If something you want to do has been done in another industry, see if you can save time by adapting it for your needs.

Chapter 8
Practise to correct errors

Practice doesn't make perfect; only perfect practice makes perfect. There's no point in practising errors but it helps to know you're correcting the right thing. So how do you know if you're practising something that will correct an issue or something that will just continue to produce errors? Organisations that have a blame or fear culture not only have the obvious cultural issues around lack of psychological safety; we believe they're also missing out on a golden opportunity to improve performance by correcting errors. To be able to do that, you need to genuinely view mistakes as data and something you can learn from to improve performance. Mistakes and failures provide organisations with live feedback, which not only helps them understand what to improve on a specific project or initiative but also where some of the systemic errors are in the organisation. Even organisations that examine their mistakes to look for learnings usually end up canvassing a bunch of opinions and generating some general themes. This can be useful to a point but to be able to effectively practise correcting errors, you need to be able to recognise the source of those errors and understand exactly how it impacts performance.

When it comes to diagnosing the source of an error, organisations seem to focus on simple cause and effect relationships. This is understandable, as the human mind tends to make straightforward links and associations. However, in organisations it can be hugely problematic because it leads to the implementation of remedies that are at best ineffective and at worst can exacerbate the problem. If a decision turns out to be wrong and poor communication is deemed the cause, everyone is sent on a communication course. But this oversimplifies the error that needs to be corrected. What was the specific communication that led to the error? And why did this happen? Were people too scared to raise concerns or too addicted to the deadline, or was a technical problem identified but not communicated in a way that decision makers could understand? If not poor communication, then perhaps it was a lack of data and so the call goes up for more data and more analysis. Again, what's the specific issue with data that led to the error and what was the impact on performance? Was the data incomplete and, if so, how did that happen? Was the data there but ignored? Because all data is open to interpretation, it's not unusual for people to dismiss some data as irrelevant when, in hindsight, it was critical.

Given all of this, there are some key considerations when dealing with errors and practising the correction of these errors to improve performance. What processes do you have in place to identify errors? Some organisations use a post-mortem or retrospectives. These can be effective if they consider the appropriate information and reach conclusions that are relevant to the improvement of performance. Often, though, the focus is on the surface of what went wrong and how to fix it without considering more systemically what was happening and why. Therefore even if you have processes in place to examine the cause of errors, you may still end up with an oversimplified cause. The first step in practising to correct errors is an accurate analysis of what the error is and how it has arisen. For this to happen, the organisational culture needs to act as a foundation and then drive to take the learning from errors rather than looking for the most straightforward explanation.

Elite sport has a culture that's almost exclusively focused on performance. As a result of this culture, coaches look at every aspect of the environment in which the individual or team operates to correct errors and maximise performance. The fact that many elite sports are televised or recorded in some form offers a good opportunity to examine the source of errors. There's also an increasing amount of data being collected in all sports to help with this analysis. For example, all football players now wear GPS tracker vests to track and measure their performance in a game. In F1, team principals have a huge amount of data to use as part of their practice to correct errors, whether they're in the set-up of a car, driver performance or race strategy. In tennis, the Hawk-Eye system, which electronically monitors the accuracy of line call decisions, is increasingly being used by players and coaches in the post-match analysis of a player's performance to identify sources of error (Takahashi et al 2023). Post-match analysis after every event focuses on what can be learned, what areas need to be changed and what needs to be practised in training or the next match. Elite sports dedicate significant amounts of time to analysing matches and races to identify errors, work out what caused them and how to correct them for the future. In football, tennis and F1, all this data helps the individual players, team coaches and managers work out where and why the errors occurred.

However, the situation in sports is far from perfect. The temptation of applying simple and cause–effect connections can still be problematic. In British football, clubs often respond to things going wrong on the pitch by firing the manager and in this respect, football isn't an exemplar. Many clubs are stuck in an endless revolving door of managers and coaching staff. These decisions are often taken to make the board look decisive or tough but the ensuing lack of stability may well be the cause of the problem. There are counter-examples in managers such as Wenger, Ferguson and Klopp, where longer-term investments can pay off in the form of sustainable performance. This can be hard to do when the stakes are high, egos are involved and there's outside scrutiny or internal pressure from fans. In some respects, the business aspect of elite sport means that people in that industry experience some of the same issues that organisations face when under pressure to perform.

Additionally, unless a sports professional is emotionally regulated and low on ego, accurately identifying errors remains a problem. Human beings don't naturally respond well to the shame of getting something wrong and this is made even worse when millions of people are watching and critiquing from their armchairs! As in organisations, this results in people not wanting to be open about or even recognise that they've made a mistake. In sport there are some good examples of humility from the likes of Gareth Southgate, Andy Murray and Lewis Hamilton but these remain rare. The ability to put aside frustration and shame enables athletes to assess their errors more accurately but it remains uncommon. This highlights that it's challenging to identify what went wrong and then be able to admit it and be open to scrutiny. To be able to identify errors accurately, you need psychological safety in the team or organisation. People need to feel safe to speak up and this is hard to achieve in a competitive environment.

We believe that correcting errors needs to go beyond sales figures, cost analysis and post-mortems and become a core part of how the organisation functions every day. Organisations usually spend nowhere near the amount of time on analysing performance and correcting errors as elite sportspeople do. They're often caught up in the addiction of being too busy and trying to perform all the time to take the time to learn. As you consider your own team or organisation, think about where and how you could build in time for your equivalent of a post-match analysis. How are you going to collect data from the day-to-day activities of your team to identify and correct errors? You may think you're too busy delivering to do this but a little will go a long way and it will pay significant dividends in the long run. To get things started, here are some of the common errors (and causes of those errors) that organisations experience, with examples of how to address them.

Lack of clarity

An ambiguous outcome or lack of clear direction can cause havoc in any organisation. There's a lot of talk in the leadership arena about the power of increased autonomy but it can quickly descend into chaos. Low levels of clarity from leadership lead to anxiety as people don't know what to do. When this happens, people do a variety of things, depending on the organisational culture and the individual personalities involved. Some people make it up, take action and hope for the best. Some do nothing, terrified of getting it wrong or being criticised, while others just do the most popular thing. You need to provide your team or organisation with a high level of clarity regarding goals and the criteria used to measure success. This means that everyone will know what to do, what matters and what will enable accurate measurement of performance. Your team will feel more empowered to perform their part and use their skills to deliver the goals autonomously.

Lack of follow-up

Keeping track of what's going on, getting progress updates and following up on things you've asked people to do should be staples of your leadership. Yet these skills are rarely taught on leadership programmes and are hard to do consistently. As a result, things get missed or leaders end up asking for detailed update reports, which take hours to write and are rarely read. The secret is in getting the balance right and having just enough follow-up to keep things moving. There are plenty of technical tools you can use to set up reminders but you must invest time in getting them to work for you. Setting up a reminder for 9 am when you're in the daily stand-up won't serve you well. Our minimum recommendation is to set aside time for follow-up and keep some kind of tracker.

Low levels of trust

It's hard to overestimate the number of errors that happen in organisations through lack of trust. If your team and organisation trust you and your leadership, they'll follow you. Being trustworthy also allows people to feel safe. From a place of safety, people can better express themselves, allow their creativity to flow, have some fun and even challenge you when they need to. Overall, this creates a great workplace culture where employees feel supported, happy, heard and inspired. However, trust is hard to develop and maintain. Leaders can't simply expect employees and colleagues to trust them implicitly from the outset. Trust is earned and developed over time and needs to be actively maintained.

To earn, develop and maintain trust you need three essential traits: honesty, consistency and integrity. You can't fake them – not for long, anyway. Keeping up a facade of honesty, consistency and integrity takes effort and you'd need to protect the facade by being defensive. What's more, in our experience people see through it. As a result, they won't trust you, even though you appear to be embodying the three essential leadership traits. If you work as a leader in any kind of collaborative situation, taking time to develop your ability to build team trust is critical.

Poor collaboration skills

Collaboration sounds nice and is an essential skill in many modern organisations but from a performance perspective it's fraught with danger. We find that it's often mistaken for consensus. In wanting to be a good collaborator, people find it hard to assess who 'should' be included, so they go broad rather than narrow, not wanting to upset anyone. This can result in the kind of groupthink that ends up in a race to the bottom for any creative idea. Involve too few people or the wrong people and you might miss some essential context or a critical viewpoint. Involve too many people and you'll end up with something uncontroversial but bland and uninteresting.

The problem with collaboration is that it can trigger all the common human dysfunctions you see play out and experience every day. These include imposter syndrome (believing you're a fraud and that others know better), people pleasing (trying to keep others happy for fear of being unpopular), fear of missing out (wanting to be involved in everything) and recency bias (being disproportionately impacted by recent events). These dysfunctions force people into a form of presenteeism where they need to be everywhere for fear of being seen as irrelevant. These dysfunctions are normal; everyone is affected by them in some way but they drive people into unhealthy collaborative behaviours that lead to systemic errors. To counteract this, organisations need to design their teams and projects well, with strong leadership and clear outcomes and deliverables. Leaders need to be able to deal with difficult emotions, set clear boundaries and help people to focus on what's important. This is all easier said than done and that's why we suggest investing in training and development in the practise phase so that leaders and managers are equipped to deal with these tricky situations.

Key takeaways

⌕ When it comes to practising to correct errors, don't try to eliminate every error or control everything. Focus on correcting the things you can correct and that will have a positive impact on performance.

⌕ Accept that there will be some areas where the effort to correct isn't worth it.

⌕ It can take a long time for organisations to correct errors, particularly if the problem is systemic.

⌕ Don't be tempted to change course every few months. This can be hard to do, especially if there are dissenting voices. Decide on a course of action and see it through.

Chapter 9
The perform phase

If your team or organisation has had the right amount and type of rest and practised the right things, then you're all set for improved performance. This section will offer ways to think about what performance means and how to organise yourself and your team to achieve it. In sports, it's easy to identify the performance you want to evaluate: it's the match or the race itself. It's clear whether you've won or lost, whether you're making progress up the rankings or sliding downwards. The performance window is the part the spectators pay to see. It seems that organisations frequently don't fully understand what it means to perform. It's usually narrowly defined and often based on sales or profit. Performance has become a buzzword in organisations and while this increased attention is positive, we've observed that the approach to it is often formulaic. The next time someone says the word 'performance', try asking them to give you the specific definition of performance in their company. You may find they're less than confident in providing it or that the definition is too general.

Sports performance can be seen as binary; you either win or you lose. That's true if your performance focus is a particular match or event. Professional sports usually view performance over a season or aim to peak at certain times of the year for key events. If your performance goal is to win a certain number of events in a year, then that's your measure. If your goal is to be in the top four of the league at the end of the season, then that's your measure. This way of thinking means that you don't overreact to one-off events during the season such as one match not going your way. In sports, leaders know that measuring performance, climbing the tennis rankings or progressing further in a tournament, going up or down the football league table and getting closer to the top of the manufacturers' table in F1 are all indicators of performance. There's a clear directional measure to performance in most sports, showing signs of progression or lack of it. Wins or losses build up to a sports professional's overall performance for a season or a year, not just whether they've won a particular event. They consider the overall goal, not just the immediacy of the win or loss of that game. We believe this is partly why sports are so much better at focusing on and measuring performance than organisations.

In organisations the word performance has become a label that people try to get excited about but can't really connect with. It's frequently stated as if just by adding the word to a project or initiative, it makes it so. To break it down, it helps to turn it from a noun (performance) into a verb (perform or performing). How do you know that you, your team or your organisation are performing? What are you measuring? What are you focusing on? To use the sporting analogy, what are people paying to see? This question helps people to connect with the meaning more easily. Performance isn't black and white but it needs clear parameters. Organisational performance goals are frequently too binary: you've either achieved it or you haven't. This is demoralising and, we believe, not conducive to sustainable performance. To truly understand your performance, the timescale over which you're evaluating it is a critical factor.

Organisations that want to become stronger culturally in terms of performance would do well to recreate this type of thinking in their business. All too often leaders overreact to what are ultimately small bumps in the road in the overall direction of travel for the organisation. With a clearer idea of what performance means to you and your organisation, the right measures to support this and by considering it over the appropriate timescale, you'll be able to focus and align your resources appropriately. This will enable you to generate the behaviours, activities, structures and processes to deliver the performance you need to meet your goals.

In essence, performance is the ability to perform a function or task. We suggest using this as your starting point. Then consider what you're trying to achieve with these functions and tasks and identify what each person in your team or area of the organisa-tion needs to do to support that performance. Which tasks need to be performed at speed, which need to be performed efficiently, which to a degree of quality or specificity and which just need to be done? Think about what performance means for your organisation. Avoid general notions of performance. There are likely to be some industry standards for doing what you're doing but what's your point of difference? What do you want to focus on? For example, performing over time (delivering a service) is different from performing to a peak (retail build-up to Christmas) and the ability to deliver a project on time and to budget. Once you're clear on your point of difference, it can help redefine what you need in terms of performance measures and activity.

The measurement of performance in a particular sport is largely defined by an external body of some kind. That body sets out the criteria for performance and the rules that need to be adhered to. There are some targets and a code of conduct for play. The code of conduct is designed to ensure consistency. Referees, both human and technological, are responsible for holding players to account. This system isn't perfect, as any commentator on football's VAR will tell you, but it's a vast improvement on the way organisations organise performance.

The challenge with performance in organisations is that the people responsible for creating the criteria and the rules are too heavily invested on a personal level. There are some best practice solutions out there but ultimately it's up to the organisation to determine the measurements of performance. Careers, livelihoods, status, ego and power all depend on proving you're performing. What's more, organisations get to create the rules for themselves. There are some obvious external parameters that organisations operate within but these are legal, defensive and designed to stop organisations making mistakes. They aren't directed towards performance. Public companies are supposedly accountable to shareholders but this accountability is largely profit driven because shareholders are primarily invested in making money. This isn't the only definition of organisational performance.

A football referee isn't invested in anything except a fair game. Ratings and systems, committees and performance goals are all attempts at creating a level playing field for performance in organisations. However, this is harder to maintain if the assessments are created within the organisation itself. This often means that behaviour around performance is messy and imperfect – and to some degree we all need to accept that. Even sports get into wrangles about refereeing decisions, steward's enquiries and line calls – and they have a reasonably good system.

When defining and evaluating performance, we recommend comparing yourself only with your peers. In sports, if you're playing in the lower leagues, there's no point in comparing yourself with a Premier League team. By all means look to them for inspiration but don't evaluate your progress against theirs. Therefore, in your organisation, consider the resources you have and the league you're playing in and evaluate your performance based on that. If you're a one-shop retailer, you can't compare yourself to the progress of a company like Amazon. You can always learn from excellence in other leagues but you should only evaluate yourself within your own. In football, you get promoted to the league above once you've performed well over a period of time. The same applies to organisations, so you need to design outcomes that are a stretch but grounded in reality.

The following chapters will explore three core concepts relating to performance in detail: how to perform towards an outcome, how to keep people focused and the importance of celebrating performance.

Key takeaways

- ⌑ Organising for performance isn't easy and will never be perfect but organisations can do it much better than they are now.
- ⌑ Define what you mean by performance for your team or organisation.
- ⌑ Set the appropriate timescales to measure your performance and avoid overreacting to small bumps in the road.

Chapter 10
Performing towards an outcome

Do you know what you're doing and why? Being busy isn't the same as performing. Are the tasks you're performing moving you towards your outcome? Worthwhile outcomes take a series of steps and a coordinated combination of people, skills and activities to achieve. They're rarely a 'to do' list. You need to organise yourself and your team towards achieving an outcome. Organisations tend to get lost in a cycle of constant structural reorganisations, which can create a sense of action and movement but don't do anything that positively contributes to performance. We've observed that these reorganisations often have more to do with solving people issues than performance, with leaders becoming fixated on discussing people rather than defining the overall strategy to improve performance. Without a well-designed strategy, you're literally moving around the deckchairs. It might be fun (for those instigating the reorganisation, not necessarily the people being constantly shuffled around) but if it's not in service of the outcome, it won't take you anywhere.

We believe that defining your outcome is the first and most important step in becoming performance focused. This is much more than a simple goal-setting exercise. In organisations, performance outcomes are ambiguous and complex. Organisational aspirations can be lofty and visionary but don't necessarily reflect the reality of the world and the environment in which you're operating. It's well worth investing time and effort in clearly defining the outcome and how it will impact performance. Company missions commonly lack clarity in terms of how to achieve them. This is fine but it's worth thinking about the internal narrative around your mission or purpose and how that translates into performance for specific areas of the organisation or even individuals. This helps employees to connect to it more closely and reminds them of what it means to perform.

To add to the complexity for leaders, performance outcomes aren't always immediately obvious. Employees, customers and even detached onlookers will make judgements about your organisation's motivations based on their own view of the world. You need to be careful to avoid the assumption that the outcome is what you assume it must be – for example, to always make money. Be careful about mind reading other people's motives. It's easy to do but if you get it wrong and act on your assumptions, you could end up creating unintended consequences that adversely affect your performance. While organisations need to have a degree of commerciality to thrive and survive, many have a wider purpose beyond profit. There are business owners who choose not to grow their business because the outcome of the business is to fund their chosen lifestyle, enable them to spend time caring, pursue a voluntary or intellectual challenge, or just because they love doing it. If you need to understand other people's motives to define your own performance outcomes, find out rather than take a guess.

There are some core mistakes we often see when people organise towards achieving an outcome. First, they're constrained by what they think they should do or how they'll be judged by others rather than what they really want or think is right. If you put a group of humans together in a room and ask them to define an outcome for organisational performance, you may not hear anything exciting. The fear of getting it wrong or being criticised often leads to bland or unambitious goals that are focused on keeping things safe and under control rather than performance.

Second, outcomes are often described as some form of comparison, for example better customer service, increased productivity or more impact. While these look positive they lack specificity and make it harder for people to understand and connect with. They also run the risk of people promoting and engaging in projects with the vague justification that they'll provide better (fill in blank here) without being clear on how this will be achieved or how it will improve performance.

Third, brainstorming sessions are commonly used for determining outcomes but can be too heavily relied upon and sometimes produce unhelpful outcomes. These sessions are only valuable if everyone feels able to contribute and speak up if they have something meaningful to add. If they're going to be useful, they'll also require a culture that embraces ideas, ambition and psychological safety. Without this, the loudest people in the room will control the agenda but the loudest people aren't necessarily the most competent or creative. Brainstorming sessions can also end up as a bit of a free-for-all, with everyone having an opinion on everything. While these sessions should open up discussion, it's also true that some people know more about certain aspects of the business than others. Think about how you can call these people forward to talk on their area of expertise, rather than just accepting all perspectives as equally valid. Everyone may have an opinion on the new performance management system but not everyone understands all the dependencies in the way your HR leaders do. Different perspectives are necessary but while they might be grounded in the knowledge of the person sharing it, they're potentially biased.

Fourth, people focus on tasks that are easy to do and exciting to be involved in but aren't relevant to achieving the outcome. It can be tempting to slip into the habit of doing what you know rather than what's necessary. You can have the fastest serve in the world but if the rest of your game isn't good enough, you'll still lose the match – unless you ace every serve. In organisations, you may have the best marketing and website in the world but if you can't deliver the product people believe they're buying, they won't be much use.

Finally, people ignore activities and roles that are put in place to protect the organisation or stop bad things from happening – what we call 'defence roles'. For some roles, performance is the absence of something rather than the achievement of something. This type of performance is valuable though perhaps not as sexy as vision setting and presenting results. A systems security manager is performing if there are no IT security problems. An employee relations leader is performing if staff complaints are being resolved quickly and fairly. These roles are often undervalued but organisations would soon know about it if the people in these roles weren't performing. Defining performance in these types of roles is essential for recognising the individuals in what are often unappreciated but essential parts of the business. The people who are successful in these areas care a great deal about their work and save the organisation an immeasurable amount of time, energy and resources by making sure things run smoothly. Be sure to remember and recognise these critical elements of your organisational performance.

Here are some essential considerations when defining solid outcomes for yourself or your organisation.

What's the purpose of what you're doing?

What's the purpose of the organisation? To be of any value, this question needs to be answered honestly. It might not be the organisation's externally stated purpose, so you might have to take a best guess and then check it out. By being clear on the organisation's purpose, you can be clear on what performance is for you or your team and how to measure it.

Creating an internal purpose statement

Mark is the CEO of an architectural organisation specialising in out-of-town development design. He took his team through this exercise and came up with 'We design and build great sheds' – shed being a term used for this type of construction. While this wouldn't make an amazing mission statement, it helped everyone in the organisation focus on what mattered, which was the quality and design of the sheds. This sent a clear message that quality and design were important, helped people to identify key areas of performance and allowed them to measure their success. Mark says the team also found it amusing and the statement became an internal mantra.

Savannah is the CEO of an organisation specialising in management training. Her team created the internal statement 'We change the culture of organisations by eliminating unintentional toxic management styles.' Their website says they provide management skills training but their internal statement directs everyone in the organisation to what matters. It defines their ideal customers, which are organisations that want to do well but have difficulties with management or inexperienced managers. To increase their impact, it also focuses their business development activities on medium or large organisations.

Savannah says that what she loves about their internal statement is that it focuses everyone, in whatever role, on what really matters. She believes it has saved them a lot of time in terms of miscommunication and misguided work.

These examples are unlikely to apply directly to your organisation but hopefully they provide you with some ideas so that you can work up an internal statement that's relevant to you and provides a clear performance outcome. It would be great if you could find an absolute measurement of some kind but don't force it. Sometimes adding a measurement that doesn't really measure properly detracts from performance because people focus only on the measurement. In larger organisations it's common for different departments to disagree on the internal statement. This is a good debate to have as there may be slightly different internal statements for different organisational areas. However, internal statements need to be aligned to the overall organisational performance outcome because any misalignment within an organisation will impede performance.

What's your part in the outcome?

Now you've grasped the bigger picture, explore your team's role in achieving this outcome. Make this as specific as possible. It's easier to be general but less helpful in shaping your outcome. Using a template sentence such as 'We do X because of Y' can be useful because it connects what you do to the why, the purpose.

Clearly defining your part

Taking Mark's example at the architectural organisation, the people sourcing the materials might say, 'We source quality materials at good prices because it means the building team can depend on the materials and won't need to compromise on quality.' The client manager might say, 'I closely track the client's expectations against the plan because being able to refine the plan or manage expectations will enable us to deliver a high-quality finish.'

In Savannah's organisation the person who designs and produces the training material might say, 'I design and produce materials that are clear and memorable because that helps managers to learn quickly and retain information.'

When do you need to perform?

In elite sports the performance point is obvious: it's the game, match or race the athlete or team are competing in. In organisations, these performance points, albeit less obvious, can be identified, and knowing where they are helps you and your team focus on the key moments that count. It will also move you and your team away from the unhelpful belief that you need to be performing all the time and support the design of the rest and practise phases of your organisational rhythm. In working through this question, look at the flow of your week, month and then year. What are the key moments in each of these? Even if you haven't paid attention to them before, you'll almost certainly know when they are. They may be the times when you're the most excited or there's a lot of energy in your team. They may be the times when you're at your most focused or the times when you think, 'I must get this one right.' Take time to think this through. The great added benefit of this is that you'll begin to see all the other times that, while necessary, don't belong in your key performance window. That regular weekly meeting might not be as important as you think and therefore you don't need to smash it.

Key takeaways

⌖ Creating an internal purpose statement and clearly defining your part in it will help provide clarity and focus.

⌖ As well as generating your overall outcome for the organisation, you can define the steps along the way and the performance points in each.

⌖ By clarifying when you need to perform, you can preserve your energy and save it for when it counts.

Chapter 11
Maintaining performance focus

Distraction is the enemy of performance. To ensure sustainability, performance takes energy and requires consistency and repetition throughout the performance window. Sadly, not every minute of it is exciting. It can be hard to stay focused, particularly if your perform phase is relatively long or you believe you need to be performing all the time. However, as a leader, doing what you can to minimise distractions will significantly benefit your overall performance as well as support the health of your team.

Do you and your team start with great energy and enthusiasm but lose energy and get distracted once it gets boring or hard? Do you forget why you started the project in the first place? Do you move on to shiny new things without finishing off the great work you started? This is a common and to some degree understandable pattern. Organisations often lose momentum in the middle of a performance window because keeping focus is so hard. This is often why teams and organisations are great in a crisis, real or imagined. Everyone rallies round, gets excited and feels the rush of doing something important and solving a problem. The same is true of the shiny new initiatives and ideas many organisations get distracted by. Consistent performance is often harder to do – it's less exciting and even dull in places and yet it's essential if you're going to perform in a sustainable way. Feeling bored, lonely, unsure of what to do next? Have a structural reorganisation, rebrand something, launch a survey, create a crisis... only joking – please don't!

Maintaining focus is easier if everyone knows the organisational outcome, their team's outcome and the key performance points they need to hit. As a leader, much of the responsibility for this focus will land at your door and rightly so. One of your key jobs is to keep yourself and those around you focused on what needs to be done to maintain performance. This isn't easy, especially when times are tough or there are many distractions. You're human too, and you're as prone to losing energy and being distracted as anyone else, which is why having a clear outcome and performance points are crucial.

Maintaining performance focus involves regularly updating your mindset. Are all the activities you planned still on track regarding the outcome? You may need to update decisions made in the light of new information. Organisations can continue with projects or services long after they're no longer relevant when the cost of quitting is perceived to be too high. Leaders know and talk about sunk costs but it's hard for human beings, especially when they're leaders and in the spotlight, to admit errors or change their minds. Consequently, even though they know in their hearts it's not working, they carry on regardless.

There are countless examples in sport of people who have continued with a tactic or game plan long after it should've been changed. There's the tennis player who keeps using a baseline strategy with an opponent when it's clearly not working or the team manager sticking with a defensive style of play that's unsuited to the opponent or the league in which they are playing. Equally, there are examples of successful sports players and managers who've had the courage to change a tactic or strategy that isn't working, even against popular opinion. The challenge is one of judgement and knowing when to stick or twist.

The same is true in organisations: there are high-profile stories of organisations that have kept going in the face of clear data suggesting they should change. There are also inspiring stories of people pushing through adversity, sticking to their strategy and ultimately creating an amazingly successful business. As a leader, you need to be clear on when you should stay focused on a clear goal and when the data is telling you that it's time to change tack. Sometimes challenges and issues are part of the performance process and sometimes they're a sign of potential failure. This can be tricky to navigate as it may feel as if your pride, status and career are on the line.

We know that making this judgement call isn't easy. There's no simple, one-size-fits-all criterion that you can employ. The best approach is to keep evaluating and surrounding yourself with people who can help you do this. Ask yourself, is it working? What's happening here? What's the data, not the feeling? Avoid getting stuck into a pattern of thinking that fuels a belief that you must make it work. It can be useful to ask yourself why you did it in the first place and whether the reason you started down this route is still valid. If so, decide to carry on while checking what, if anything, you need to change. If not, what needs to happen? Ask trusted colleagues to keep you honest.

There are times to stand back and get a wider perspective on your progress and times when you must focus only on what's happening in the here and now. Leaders can get lost in examining all the potential consequences to the point that it affects performance in the moment. Tennis coaches teach professional players to think only about the point they're playing. If you're losing and your attention is drawn too much to the big picture, you can lose focus and the chances of losing get higher. In F1 on race day, the whole team is set up to allow the driver to focus on their driving and not get distracted by issues with the car or other external factors. In organisational life, we recommend that the best strategy is to stand back to get an overall perspective, decide whether you're on track, then get your head down and focus. This takes discipline because people usually have a natural preference and therefore default to that, especially under pressure. However, you can train yourself to intentionally take on a different mindset or ask someone who naturally does it to help you.

Here are some key considerations for maintaining focus in the performance window.

How do you know you're on track?

Find a way of monitoring whether your performance is on track to achieve your outcome. Finding the right data to monitor performance is part of this. It must be data that, based on the outcomes you designed, measures performance towards those chosen outcomes. But data, however useful, isn't the only useful reference point. You may want to monitor what's happening inside the organisation itself. For example, does everyone seem too frantic? Does there appear to be more noise around the organisation than normal? Does the data you have match with what you feel and sense is happening? One other factor to consider is your previous experience. What normally happens that negatively impacts performance? You're likely to know what that is, so watch out for it and monitor it. Don't just hope or assume it will be different this time.

Try to avoid comparing yourself to things that don't matter, such as irrelevant competition or people you know in other organisations. Comparisons are only useful if you can learn from their mistakes or successes. Be careful about making judgements about what these comparisons tell you. In our experience, there are likely to be many things you don't know for sure about other companies and this could lead you to reach the wrong conclusion about where you are in relation to your outcome and your competitors.

Motivation

Maintaining motivation is a fundamental contributor to maintaining focus. Unmotivated people will get distracted and this can waste a lot of time and effort. The best form of motivation in performance is intrinsic motivation: an internal drive or sense of purpose. People who are intrinsically motivated will require less oversight and will be happy to keep going because there's something about what they're doing that naturally drives them.

People who are extrinsically motivated, for example those who are doing an activity to obtain external recognition or reward, require a lot more from their leaders to remain focused and perform consistently. This is why recruiting people who truly love their work for its own sake is critical to organisational performance. If you're trying to keep people focused and your whole day is spent following up, providing support and validating work, you'll be exhausted. All responsible leaders need to do some of this but leaders with several extrinsically motivated people in their teams will get drained quickly. It's harder to maintain performance in these situations and you can end up spending too much of your time managing people's issues rather than working towards your outcomes.

Be alert for distractions

During a performance window, you ideally want to keep people's minds on what they really need to do. Try to avoid letting them drift off into someone else's area of work or having new, alternative ideas. Your leadership is essential here as the process of performing can be tough, unrewarding or unexciting at times. It's easy to get distracted by a louder problem, your boss's shiny new idea or something you're more easily able to measure or do. It would be better to help people narrow their focus so that they have the maximum amount of brain power available to keep performing towards the outcome.

Changing ways of working during a performance window

Under team leader Raj's supervision, an innovative design company changed their ways of working to support the team's ability to focus during the performance window. First, they avoid all meetings and events not directly related to the work – this means no company meetings, training, team building, off-sites or development conversations. This helps the team avoid getting distracted by peripheral topics. Instead, Raj encourages them to increase the number of connection points on topics directly related to the work: daily stand-ups, focused one-to-ones, informal group huddles. When logistically possible and to make collaboration easier, Raj moves everyone into one physical space. To make it sustainable, the leadership team rotates responsibility for maintaining focus.

Understanding your team and yourself

Knowing your team well will pay dividends in the performance window. By understanding what drives your people, their life situations, their interests and their working styles, you can shortcut a lot of communication. Team building is an essential consideration for the rest and practise phases, so that the team can simply perform in the performance window. We believe that now is not the time for you to get to know the team; this work should already have been done. You don't want to use valuable time and emotional energy teaching people how to work with each other. When the pressure is on, people issues will have a disproportionate impact on performance so they need to be mitigated before you get going.

Maintaining focus can also be stressful and that's another reason for doing your own personal development work in the other phases. If you know what your stress triggers are in the performance window, prioritise working on these in the rest or practise phases, so that you aren't drained or distracted by them. For leaders who receive coaching, their coach usually supports them to stay focused during the performance window because the real change work is done in the rest or practise phase.

Where the performance window is relatively short, providing they have time to rest afterwards, people can cope with the intensity. If the window is longer, you'd do well to consider how to make it sustainable. It may be possible to rotate responsibilities or provide short rest and practise phases to provide some respite and help people remain focused. In football, managers often rotate their squad when they have a long season or several intense matches in a short period of time to maintain the overall team performance.

Key takeaways

⊠ Keeping your team or organisation focused during this phase will require you to do the same. If you get easily distracted, bored or push through to an outcome without adequately evaluating whether it's still the right one, then make it a priority to develop these skills in the practise phase.

⊠ For a lot of leaders, the performance window is challenging. It can be exciting, draining, dull, monotonous, fulfilling and frustrating all at the same time.

⊠ If you don't do the requisite amount of personal development work in the rest or practise phases, you can end up doubting yourself, getting drained by the effort involved or simply giving up.

⊠ Leaders who know themselves well and have good coping strategies in place are more likely to hit their outcomes and do it with some energy left in the tank for cele-brations.

Chapter 12
Celebrating performance

Celebrations are rites of passage – they acknowledge the achievement and recognise the skill and dedication involved in achieving something beyond the norm. Celebrations are much more than simply having fun – they're a critical part of the rest, practise, perform approach. However, to be effective, we believe they need to be appropriate and targeted.

Celebrations form a core element of elite sports: cups, medals and throwing champagne over each other are all important parts of the performance. If you think these types of celebrations are over the top, you might be right. They can appear excessive or even slightly ridiculous but they do perform an essential role in the personal motivation of the individuals and in the commercial viability of sports as a profession. Sports celebrations are also about prestige. The winners are declared the best, even if that's for one day or one year. This isn't just about a good feeling. In most sports, you only get highly paid if you're at the top of the sport and there's usually a steep incline at the top end. Celebrating publicly as people progress is essential, as doing so tells the world to pay attention to this person, that they've achieved something impressive, that they have potential. In sport this can attract important sponsorship and other rewards such as public appearances, which are critical in a world where the career peak can be short. We think organisations could learn a lot from how sports celebrate progress and potential, specifically focusing on how to reward appropriately and the type of celebration required.

Organisations struggle to celebrate performance in the right way and that's partly because the definition of performance is frequently vague. If you don't know if you've performed, how can you celebrate it? It's hard to feel the elation sports professionals experience after a win. Leaders and teams can be so exhausted and relieved to have got through the performance window that they don't make the time or have the energy to organise an appropriate celebration. As a result, employees often report that awards, recognition schemes and parties all feel a bit fake or frivolous. Organisations may never be able to match the high-octane celebrations of sports professionals but we believe there's scope for improvement. Celebrating performance isn't just a nice thing to do. It programs people's minds to seek more. The dopamine release that sportspeople experience in celebrating wins motivates them to keep going as well as building their confidence.

Performance celebrations also provide an opportunity to unpack what went well and what can be replicated in future. This is something organisations frequently miss out on. Modelling excellence is a great way to improve performance. If something has worked well, identify the success factors and explore ways to integrate them into future work. It will rarely just be down to hard work or even luck; there will be key repeatable elements that created the success. As such, it's an opportunity to learn and improve as well as celebrate.

Celebrations mark a change of phase – an ending, a completion. Organisations that simply move on to the next thing not only miss the opportunity to celebrate but they also run the risk of demotivating their team. This leads to an increased likelihood that some people will burn out, believing that they need to keep going in a never-ending cycle of performing. Creating a culture where performance is celebrated reduces these risks. Here are some key considerations for celebrating performance that we believe would be beneficial for all organisations.

Take the opportunity to model performance excellence

Organisations would benefit from carefully examining why something went well just as much as when something went wrong – and then celebrating it. An element of luck, when something good happens by chance, is common in success stories. To model performance excellence you must distinguish between luck and the excellent things you did. Being able to make this distinction enables you to recreate and even improve performance in the future. It also allows you to celebrate the right things and draw attention to them for others to learn from.

Humans aren't great at acknowledging that luck or fortunate but random chains of events are a factor in their success. Success stories are written in hindsight, where facts and perspectives can be linked together in a way that makes it all look as if it was deliberately planned and executed. In modelling your own excellence, you'll be able to untangle the two and focus on replicating the key components you can control or influence. Examples of luck are fortunate timings, events you haven't predicted, help you didn't seek or ask for, or the failure of the competition. Examples of excellence are your skills and abilities, your ability to plan and organise projects and people, your ability to accurately predict something key to success, the quality of teamwork and your skill in creating clear goals and objectives. Having identified the areas of excellence, examine what you did in the rest or practise phases and how that led to a successful outcome. Then replicate all of this in future in other projects or parts of the organisation.

Discovering and calling out excellence

In Mark's architectural organisation, it was standard practice to complete post-project reviews. These forensic examinations covered everything from team communication and customer service to how supplies were acquired and costs negotiated. To avoid bias and maximise the opportunities for learning across the company, the review was carried out by a partner not involved in the project itself.

The partner would prepare a report on the key learnings and standout successes of the project and present it to all the other partners. In the review meeting, the partners would decide which learnings to act on, what reward or celebration was appropriate for the successes and how to build on them. The review partner had to prove the successes were because of skill or excellence, either by an individual or the whole team. These were frequently incorporated in learning programmes and future mentoring sessions and written up as company stories displayed around the office so that everyone could learn from them.

Design the appropriate celebration

It can be tempting to have broad-brush celebrations in the perceived interest of fairness but this removes the light from the key contributors to performance. There are ways to celebrate specific achievements without compromising on fairness. You just need clear and consistent criteria.

Consider what you do to celebrate performance in your organisation. The celebration should be proportionate and appropriate – there's no need to high five every well-written email. Decide what's expected and what's exceptional in your organisation and design the celebration to suit. There's no right or wrong way to do it but if you've defined what performance means to you as well as your performance outcomes, it should be easier to do. Organisations that understand the importance of celebrations and do them well have multiple ways to celebrate different types of achievements: long service (if that's important), a spot bonus for small but exceptional pieces of work, name checks in company announcements for unique contributions. Whatever criteria you decide to use, think through how you can apply these as consistently and fairly as possible.

When you celebrate, be clear about what, specifically, you're celebrating and ensure it sends the right message to the rest of the organisation. Be careful with this, as your message will send a signal about the culture within your organisation. If all you celebrate is heroic effort, long hours and success despite adversity, that's what you'll get more of. This may be needed in a project or organisational situation but if it's a repeating pattern, something's wrong in the organisation. Celebrate projects that went smoothly and efficiently as this is likely to be a sign of excellence. If you value teamwork over individual contributions, then be sure to acknowledge and celebrate that.

Some aspects of performance should be rewarded rather than celebrated. The key difference is the way you acknowledge it. If you don't publicly acknowledge performance, it's a reward rather than a celebration. This is neither good nor bad but understanding the difference will help you decide what falls into a reward system and what requires a celebration. As a general guide, reward people for doing their job well and celebrate excellence beyond that or a unique achievement. This helps people to distinguish between what's expected and what's exceptional. Rewards feed people's intrinsic motivation – they feel good about themselves and their work but the feeling of satisfaction isn't reliant on other people congratulating them or knowing how good they are. They may choose to tell others about their reward but it isn't the same as an authority figure publicly calling it out.

Celebrating team success

In Savannah's training organisation, teamwork was highly valued. The delivery team might be the people in front of the clients but the team behind the scenes made the magic happen. Savannah only celebrated successes as a team. Individual contributions were recognised via bonuses, quietly and with no fanfare. When a client project scored highly on feedback or they were invited back to do more work, everyone who had any touchpoint with that client was given a budget for their own celebration. They could choose what they wanted to do: go for a meal, see a show or take a spa day. She also decided to celebrate each team member. On their birthdays, each member of the team received a shoutout and a gift chosen by the rest of the team. These simple strategies ensured there was consistency and clarity around the purpose of celebrations.

Feed it forward

Once the celebrations are over, decide how you're going to build on this success in the future. Sometimes it's more of the same activities but often not. Are you trying to get to the next league? Are you trying to scale? Use this opportunity to define your next outcome; don't just aim for incremental improvements. It may be a one-off, never to be repeated thing. However, if your performance windows run in cycles, think about how what you've learned can inform future cycles. This could be information about your product or external competition. It could also be useful to examine what you've learned about yourself, your team and your ability to run the rest, practise, perform approach.

Key takeaways

- ¤ There's much to be gained from well-designed and appropriate celebrations in organisations.
- ¤ The rush to move onto the next thing can be almost compulsive, particularly in organisations where celebrating is viewed as something frivolous and a bit distasteful.
- ¤ Some leaders also fear that celebrating will make people lazy, rest on their laurels or 'get too big for their boots'. This may happen but it will be a signal of an individual's own personality or a cultural issue rather than a direct result of the celebration.
- ¤ Overlooking or dismissing celebrations of performance isn't just demotivating. It can be a contributor to burnout, as people won't be getting the sense of purpose and achievement they need from their work.
- ¤ Celebrating performance provides opportunities to build on your success, model excellence and feed it forward into future phases.
- ¤ Well-thought-through celebrations should leave you and your team with energy and enthusiasm for the next adventure – maybe after a well-earned rest.

Chapter 13
The real world

On paper, leading an organisation is quite straightfor-ward. But in practice, it isn't as easy. Hopefully, much of what you've read in this book makes sense. You will no doubt already know some of it. But have you put it into action? And if you have, have you done it repeatedly, consciously and purposely? In our experience, the greatest challenge for leaders in organisations is not that they don't know what to do; it's that they don't do it consistently and don't know whether it's taking them anywhere. We get it; it's hard to know whether something is working or not. In organisational life, time is rarely on your side. As a result of external pressure, leaders frequently have the tendency to go against their own judgement, even if they know it's wrong to do so.

If you like the ideas in this book but are still sceptical about whether it's possible to implement them, you won't be alone. You're probably thinking about the permission you might need, what people will think of you, how you'll convince other people or how you'll know whether you're on the right track. Will people even believe you when you highlight the importance of the rest phase? Will people get impatient in the practise phase and want to push on? Will you spend time in endless meetings trying to get people to agree on your definition of performance?

This is the reality of working in an organisation. It can be hard to go against 'the way we do it here'. It's probably easier not to rock the boat. Remember, though, that you invested your time and attention into reading this book for a reason – and that reason probably has something to do with feeling a little dissatisfied with the status quo and frustrated with some aspect of your organisation's performance. Remember that it *is* possible. This is how elite sportspeople organise themselves. There's evidence that this approach works – you're not attempting something that's never been tried before. There are nuances and differences between sports and organisations but there are also many similarities.

The key to successful implementation of these ideas is to pace the organisation from its current state to where you want to go. We recommend that you focus your attention on the areas that matter most to performance, conduct a pilot to test new ways of working, analyse the results and build from there.

Pace your organisation

Even if you love some of the suggestions in this book, bear in mind that your organisation may not be ready to act on them. Think about which ideas will land best, given the current state of your organisation and the mindset of your leaders and colleagues. If you currently work in an organisation where there are budget constraints, suggesting retreats, increasing your L&D portfolio and planning big celebrations probably won't be well received. It might be better to tweak some of what you already have in place rather than embark on a big programme of change.

However, if you have full autonomy and want to go full speed ahead, proceed with caution. Remember that your teams may not be ready for a huge shift in their ways of working. Even positive changes can be met with suspicion and resistance, so make sure you take the time to explain why you're doing what you're doing, work through the ideas with others, take it step by step and bring people along with you. Organisations seem to be in a constant state of change and the latest trend is to talk about 'change fatigue'. In your organisation, we suggest thinking about these actions as developments, improvements or ways of moving forward and talking about them as such.

Focus on what matters most

We understand that it can be tempting to grab new ideas and run with them but that can result in a less than optimal implementation and you can end up with a random and inconsistent outcome. Instead, think about two or three key adjustments you believe will make the most difference to performance. This could be as simple as defining performance. In a service organisation or one with an intangible output, defining performance isn't easy but hugely powerful. Don't be tempted to go for quick wins unless they significantly impact performance. Psychologically, people love quick wins because they feel like progress. But sometimes that progress is false or unsustainable. You might disregard some ideas because they're too challenging or not possible at this time – and that's fine. Just try to avoid a scenario where you convince yourself something impacts performance because it's easy to do.

Run a test pilot

In the spirit of practising what we preach, we recommend running a test pilot as the ultimate form of practise phase. If you're doing something very different from how you currently operate, a test pilot will enable you to practise in a safe and controlled way and help you convince others that what you're suggesting works for your organisation. By their nature, test pilots are usually small in scale, so pick a small group of people or a small project to test. You don't want to run a test pilot on your organisation's most business-critical project. Manage it carefully and track what's working and where improvements are needed. Give it enough time. Involve all the people in the test and feedback loop. Once you have a successful test pilot, you'll be ready to roll it out on a larger scale.

The rest, practise, perform mindset

Rest, practise, perform is as much a mindset as it is an approach. You can implement the concepts formally but you can also adopt the three phases as a way of thinking about how you work – and even how you live your life. Leaders can make significant progress simply by role modelling the right type of rest and the right type of practice. Leaders who engage fully with their L&D requirements will get more out of the practise phase than leaders who don't. Leaders who take a little bit more time to define performance in straightforward terms will do better than those who don't. Leaders who hold the appropriate types of celebration and reward people in the right way will have more motivated teams than those who don't.

If you love a particular sport, go and study it. Notice how the athlete or team you support implements the rest, practise, perform approach in their field. It's always easier, not to mention more fun, to understand and implement something you have a close connection with. It's also more meaningful to you personally. You may learn even more that you can apply and adapt into your work. Scrutinise how they mentally prepare for performance, how they deal with setbacks, how they solve problems, how they communicate – these are all transferable from sport into organisations like yours.

Finally, it's time to move on from the old 100 per cent, 24/7 performance mindset. We hope we've convinced you that this mindset doesn't work and is unsustainable – but you probably knew that already. Instead, learn from elite sports and create a rest, practise, perform rhythm in your organisation. It is possible to achieve great things and have a healthy workforce – and now you know how to do it.

References

Ahola, K, Toppinen-Tanner, S & Seppänen, J (2017) 'Interventions to alleviate burnout symptoms and to support return to work among employees with burnout: Systematic review and meta-analysis.' *Burnout Research* 4. URL: doi.org/10.1016/j.burn.2017.02.001

Almatrooshi, B, Singh, S K & Farouk, S (2016) 'Determinants of organizational performance: a proposed framework.' *International Journal of Productivity and Performance Management* 65(6). URL: doi.org/10.1108/IJPPM-02-2016-0038

Aronsson, G, Theorell, T et al (2017) 'A systematic review including meta-analysis of work environment and burnout symptoms'. *BMC Public Health* 17.

Cartwright, S & Cooper, C (2009) *The Oxford Handbook of Organizational Well-being*. Oxford University Press.

Finan, S, McMahon, A & Russell, S (2022). '"At what cost am I doing this?" An interpretative phenomenological analysis of the experience of burnout among private practitioner psychotherapists'. *Counselling and Psychotherapy Research* 22 URL: doi.org/10.1002/capr.12483

Fletcher, D & Arnold, R (2011) 'A qualitative study of performance leadership and management in elite sport'. *Journal of Applied Sport Psychology* 23(2). URL: doi.org/10.1080/10413200.2011.559184

Foy, T, Dwyer, R et al (2019) 'Managing job performance, social support and work-life conflict to reduce workplace stress'. *International Journal of Productivity and Performance Management* 68(6). URL: doi.org/10.1108/IJPPM-03-2017-0061

Jo, J & Ellingson, J (2019) 'Social relationships and turnover: A multidisciplinary review and integration'. *Group Organization Management* 44(2). URL: doi.org/10.1177/1059601119834407

Konkel, M & Heffernan, M (2022) 'How job insecurity affects emotional exhaustion: A study of job insecurity rumination and psychological capital during COVID-19.' *The Irish Journal of Management* 40(2). URL: doi.org/10.2478/ijm-2021-0009

Maslach, C, Schaufeli, W et al (2001) 'Job burnout'. *Annual Review of Psychology* 52.

Mind (2022) 'Mental health facts and statistics'. URL: mind.org.uk/information-support/types-of-mental-health-problems/statistics-and-facts-about-mental-health/how-common-are-mental-health-problems

Pijpker, R, Vaanager, L et al (2021) 'Seizing and realizing the opportunity: A salutogenic perspective on rehabilitation after burnout'. *Work* 68(3). URL: doi.org/10.3233/WOR-203393

Salminen, S, Andreou, E et al (2017) 'Narratives of

burnout and recovery from an agency perspective: A two-year longitudinal study.' *Burnout Research* 7. URL: doi.org/10.1016/j.burn.2017.08.001

Sethibe, T & Steyn, R (2015) 'The relationship between leadership styles, innovation and organisational performance: A systematic review'. *South African Journal of Economic and Management Sciences* 18(3). URL: doi.org/10.4102/sajems.v18i3.1193

Sfreddo, L, Vieira, G et al (2021) 'ISO 9001 based quality management systems and organisational performance: a systematic literature review.' *Total quality management & business excellence* 32(3–4). URL: doi.org/10.1080/14783363.2018.1549939

Supej, M & Spörri, J (2021) 'Special issue on "Sports performance and health"'. *Applied Sciences* 11(6). URL: doi.org/10.3390/app11062755

Takahashi, H, Okamura, S & Murakami, S (2023) 'Performance analysis in tennis since 2000: A systematic review focused on the methods of data collection'. *International Journal of Racket Sports Science* 4(2). URL: doi.org/10.30827/Digibug.80900

Useful links

Motorsport: motorsport.com/f1/news/what-is-f1-summer-break-why-does-it-happen-how-long

Professional Football Scout Association: thepfsa.co.uk/when-does-the-football-season-start-and-end

The kaizen approach: kaizen.com/what-is-kaizen

About the authors

Before they set up Monkey Puzzle Training & Consultancy in 2007, Karen Meager and John McLachlan both enjoyed successful careers in business. While studying for her MBA, Karen became fascinated by the psychological make-up of people who are great at what they do and used her knowledge to recruit and train for all types of roles in her organisation, from call centres and sales to leaders. John had always been more interested in people than accounting and used his warm sense of humour and depth of understanding to help businesses and business owners be successful and live more fulfilling lives.

Karen and John take the latest scientific and academic thinking and make it useful and easy to apply. Their approach is grounded in research and professional practice that spans Karen and John's 20-plus year careers. They both have multiple Masters degrees in psychology and health research. Karen's specialist research area is mental health and burnout in organisations, while John has researched what organisations can learn from elite sports performance. The combination of their research led to the rest, practise, perform approach that is the focus of this book. They integrate this thinking into their own experience, business understanding and psychological training to make it practical and easy to understand and apply. Their goal is for people to bring more of themselves to their lives, make their lives easier and be successful in whatever they choose to do.

**For more information,
go to monkeypuzzletraining.co.uk**